Condemned Again

Condemned Again

Skhumbuzo Letlaka

Copyright © 2015 by Skhumbuzo Letlaka.

ISBN: Softcover   978-1-4990-9371-1
          eBook   978-1-4990-9372-8

All rights reserved. No part of this book may be reproduced or transmitted in any form or by any means, electronic or mechanical, including photocopying, recording, or by any information storage and retrieval system, without permission in writing from the copyright owner.

Any people depicted in stock imagery provided by Thinkstock are models, and such images are being used for illustrative purposes only.
Certain stock imagery © Thinkstock.

Print information available on the last page.

Rev. date: 09/03/2015

To order additional copies of this book, contact:
Xlibris
800-056-3182
www.Xlibrispublishing.co.uk
Orders@Xlibrispublishing.co.uk
701112

Contents

Preface 7
Abbreviations 11
Dramatis Personae 13
Introduction 15

1   The Secret Minutes 19
2   The Unbanning of the Liberation Movements 21
3   Reality for the 'Inxiles' 28
4   The Persistence of Racism 32
5   I Stand Accused Again 38
6   The Land Question 41
7   Education and the Shortage of Skills 44
8   Africa Needs New Rulers 48
9   All Power to the People 53
10 Inequality amongst Races 58
11 Blame It on the Whites 63
12 Nelson Mandela, the Saint 69
13 Crime 72
14 The Problem Child 77

Conclusion 85
Bibliography 89

Preface

The birth of this piece of work emanated from my own frustrations and that of many other comrades who have been largely disappointed by the new South African political dispensation. Our struggle for liberation (to be candid) has been a fruitless exercise. We feel pity as we observe the failure of our government. Poor people still live below the breadline. Foreigners such as Somalis, Ethiopians, Pakistanis—some of whom will enter this country as refugees—are given priority in business ventures against black South Africans. I am further perturbed by the lack of commitment on the side of our government; after twenty years of our freedom, our people are still trapped in the vicious cycle of poverty, in slums and squatter camps, and lack of service delivery and prioritisation of our municipalities in a country which is richer than a number of rich nations in the world.

We are disturbed by the lack of leadership and accountability in the key areas of development and by the corruption from the president to the lowest official in the government. We inherited a country with the best infrastructure in the continent and the developing world, and yet we seem to be regressing instead of making progress. What exacerbates the situation is seeing the people who were collaborating with the enemy, fence-sitters who were always claiming to be neutral, and reactionary elements who were assisting the enemy to arrest, kill, and maim us; all of them are enjoying the fruits of the freedom we fought for. We further protest in silence as they hold senior positions in our movement, the ANC; in local governments as councillors; in the provincial parliaments; and in the national legislature as MPs.

We continue to lament in silence as we observe our former oppressors enjoying the freedom of exploiting us anew. They get away with murder in the farms, where they continue to exploit black peasants, dragging them with their vans, killing, and feeding them to the lions; they commit murder with impunity and portray arrogance by throwing African dwellers out of what they call 'their farms'. We stand dumbfounded and perturbed by the continued economic dominance of the white race in our country, where the old apartheid oligarchy still enjoys the privileges of their own without sharing the wealth with the Africans, the indigenous people of the land. They control all the strategic and economically viable areas of our country and replicate apartheid's economic and business status quo, which continues to keep black business talent at bay.

The ANC has been a serious disappointment. In Durban, my hometown, they have allowed the dominance of Asians and had sacrificed black people at the altar of the vicious cycle of poverty. The ANC has become a den of scoundrels, and they have sold the future of our people to the white and Indian cabals; they are playing second fiddle to these races while begging with cap in hand for the donations and crumbs that are offered by the businesses of these cabals and the politics of patrons and clients. These races are devouring a lion's share of our local economy; they continue to feed on the blood and sweat of the African majority, while the scoundrels of the ANC enjoy the remnants.

The ANC has crafted new strategies which are very similar to the ones used by the apartheid regime. They sidelined black intellectuals and intelligent UDF activists from the centre, thus making jokes of the black buffoons in the metro area and local municipalities, who can neither read nor write. Point Road in Durban is a hub of drugs and prostitution of our daughters, and yet the intelligence agencies are monitoring the old UDF activists and ensuring that they are frustrated and kept away from employment and strategic positions where they can influence change. Illiterate people are made fun of. They are placed in senior positions in local governments and in the South African Broadcasting Corporation (SABC), some of whom have lied about their academic qualifications. Intelligent comrades who suffered in apartheid jails are pushed to the periphery, while the clowns are paid salaries of kings and queens.

Here is an injustice I have seen in the world—an injustice caused by rulers, stupid people are given positions of authority while the rich are ignored. I have seen slaves on horseback while noblemen go on foot like slaves. (Ecclesiastes 10:5–6)

> The DA must be enjoying the last laugh, and the National Party must have given the ANC a very good coaching clinic, and they are doing the dirty jobs for their masters, par excellence.

As we mourn the death of our society, the Book of Lamentations in the Bible sums it up in these few words:

Remember, O Lord, what has come to us and see our reproach. Our property and inheritance has been turned over to strangers; our homes have been given over to aliens. We have become orphans, without fathers: our mothers now are as widows. We must pay for the water we drink: our wood we secure at high cost. Our pursuers now sit on our necks: we toil without rest. To get food to stay alive, we went begging to [other *races*]. We are ruled by those who are no better than slaves and no one can save us from their power. With peril to our lives we secure bread. Our skin is as hot as an oven. Happiness has gone out of our lives; grief has taken the place of our dances. Nothing is left of all we were proud of, we are oppressed and now we are doomed. We are sick at our very hearts and can hardly see through our tears. (A shortened version of Lamentations 5)

You can fool some people, but you cannot fool them all the time. The ANC is still going to enjoy power and the gravy train for quite some time. The presidents we've seen so far leave much to be desired.

President Mandela inherited the economy which was taking a nosedive and a country which was teetering on the brink of the abyss. He had no clear economic policies, and he contradicted himself on numerous occasions to the international investors. He spoke about nationalisation when the entire world was moving away from this economic taboo. He was still clinging to the 1955 archaic clauses of the Freedom Charter.

Then came Thabo Mbeki; he introduced the GEAR as the turnaround strategy. Although the alliance partners were up in arms in showing their vehement opposition to this policy, it worked very well for the holders of the means of production, and there was a trickle down to the poor; his hired US and European technocrats assisted him to the fullest.

Jacob Zuma says he is a loyal servant of the ANC, and he works with the collective. This is a gently way of saying *angazi madoda* (which means 'I don't know'). Although Mr Trevor Manuel has drafted the NDP, which has been adopted by the ANC in Jacob Zumas's term of office, no one can tell you the name of the present economic policy precisely because we are dealing with his corruption cases all the time than analysing the economic policies. Jacob Zuma has become a liability to the ANC and the country at large, an embarrassment to the Zulus as the largest tribe. Whosoever is giving him advice should tell him to get off at the next bus stop while he can still preserve a shred of his dignity.

It is better to have wise people reprimand you than to have stupid people sing your praises. (Ecclesiastes 7:5)

> Perhaps this is a lesson worth learning because if the ANC does not learn from these mistakes, this country is going to the dogs.

ABBREVIATIONS

ANC – African National Congress
COSATU – Congress of South African Trade Union
CODESA – Convention for a Democratic South Africa
SACP – South African Communist Party
UDF – United Democratic Front
PAC – Pan-Africanist Congress
NP – National Party
EFF – Economic Freedom Fighters
HOD – House of Delegates

Dramatis Personae

Allan Boesak
Amilcar Cabral
Archie Gumede
Angie Motshekga
Albertina Sisulu
Bheki Cele
Baleka Mbete
Chombe
F. W. de Klerk
Floyd Shivambu
Gwen Mahlangu-Nkabinde
Hendrik Verwoerd
Helen Zille
Julius Malema
Jacob Zuma
John Dube
kaMadiba
Lindiwe Mazibuko
maNgema
Mbongeni Ngema
maNtuli
Mobutu Sese Seko
Nelson Mandela
Patrice Lumumba
Pixley ka Seme
Thabo Mbeki
Thandi Modise
Walter Sisulu
Winnie Madikizela-Mandela

INTRODUCTION

At the outset, it will be worthwhile to start by pointing out that writing a book of this nature needs someone with courage and guts to confront the realities that many writers choose to ignore, using the type of language that avoids concreteness of the subject. This book is based on my experiences and the way in which I grew up under the apartheid in South Africa and the campaigns that we chose to engage in as we influenced the liberation struggle. We fought for our freedom, and we liberated ourselves through our joint efforts in the United Democratic Front (UDF), which was led by Allen Boesak, Albertina Sisulu, and Archie Gumede respectively.

When you write a book on politics, you are not producing a work of art; the debunking motive exposes the lie and tells the truth as it is perceived by the writer. The facts are inexplicably linked to the perception of the writer and his or her translation and interpretation of the situation as it presents itself. There are always two sides to a story though, and the first side sounds true until the other one presents a different version. The only quandary any ruling party can face would be that of accepting criticism and dealing with the facts presented in the book or simply choosing to be in denial and dismissing the argument as intellectual hogwash and useless garbage. The truth might not augur very well, but bitter as it may sound, it has to be told.

They say politics is a dirty game, and I agree with those who think this way. We have seen many bad things in South African politics; we have seen the dirty linen being hung outside for everyone to see. We have witnessed men of good standing going down, and it became business as usual, like nothing had happened. Politics has taken down many leaders of good reputation and replaced them with dictators, despots, and tyrants. Politics continues to meddle into the lives of decent people, and it has continued to destroy managerialism and professionalism in the entire establishment.

Today we have people of good standing in our country—both men and women—protesting against corruption and rampant nepotism in the departments of a new government. The archbishop emeritus of the Anglican Church Archbishop Tutu has vowed not to vote for the ruling party again; he has repeated this as a clarion call to all South Africans, insisting that if they are truly committed to prosperity and future stability of their country, they should vote for another party. There are many other prominent figures in our communities who have developed this attitude and apathy. As we were approaching the election in 2014, Mr Ronnie Kasrils and Ms Nozizwe Madlala-Routledge, stalwarts of the ANC, openly encouraged people not to vote for the ANC. They started a campaign of spoiling papers in the ballot box. Many decent South Africans are fed up with the ANC and their way of governing.

This is not to say that the mistakes of the ANC have climaxed to the point of no return; there is still hope. The Book of Ecclesiastes in chapter nine verse four states: 'Better is the living dog than a dead lion.' We can still see our country being represented in the international arena by the calibre that matches that of developed countries, and we can still see our communities being represented by leaders by their own choice and not the ones appointed from the regional offices of the ruling party or the type of leaders with a *baaskap* mentality, who will dance to the tune of a clique of leaders not elected by the people. Improvements can be seen in environments where the social space is opened for our intellectuals to freely express themselves and come up with new ideas that can propel our country to the pedestals of the First World.

When the ANC stops the killings that are going on within, the rebirth of the ANC we know might bring back some new hopes. People who have no clue of what politics is all about are leading the branches, and they do this because leading a branch is a ticket to opulence. It gives the leader some control and access to the state tenders and some upward mobility within the party, and it creates high hopes that anyone can become a big leader or even a president regardless of the level of their education. These are the experiences that we come across at the branch levels of the ANC as they continue to boast about the power of the branch. Once they show some determination to deal with these problems, maybe they will be able to win back the respect of all South Africans as they once had.

There are gatekeepers in the branches of the ANC, and they have no understanding of the programs of this movement. The ANC has documents such as Through the Eye of the Needle, Strategy and Tactics, the Freedom Charter, and the Constitution of the ANC. All these documents are spelling clearly what this movement is all about, and they are clearly elaborating on how individuals should behave. There is no cadre in the ANC who would ever think of eliminating another comrade if he has fully understood what these documents are saying. What we find today is Operation Elimination, and comrades are killing one another for positions.

Another noticeable pitfall is that the ANC is event oriented. Members will be called by a loud hailer to the meeting, they will be told about a coming event, and they will be asked to attend the events. They will be toyi-toying (freedom songs and dance), and then they will listen to the shallow speakers and go back home as blank as they came. The behaviour of our leaders needs some serious attention; if it continues like that, the ANC will be left with the people who have never been to school, who are killers, muggers, tenderpreneurs, and opportunists who have no record on good governance or no struggle credential.

Time doesn't wait for them. There are groups in the opposition, and all of them are capitalising on the weaknesses of the ruling party. They are making inroads into the strongholds of the ANC. The trade unions in the mining sector, especially in the platinum mines, are organising against the unions that are affiliated with the Congress of South African Trade Union (COSATU), the federation in alliance with the ANC. There are civil organisations, such as Mazibuye in Durban, which are beginning to ask questions that should have long been addressed by the ANC if they are to avoid the tensions amongst the racial groups in South Africa and the dominance of the Asians in eThekwini Municipality.

There are new parties which are formed by leaders with clear struggle credentials, leaders who are beginning to take up the gauntlet; they pose questions that are mind-boggling. Some of these leaders have never been members of the ruling party, and they did not reject the ANC from within. They did not leave the ruling party out of anger as the excuse will be made about the UDM and COPE.

Former Youth League leader Mr Julius Malema has formed a new party, the Economic Freedom Fighters (EFF), which is aimed at addressing the economic freedom in our lifetime (as they say), and all these efforts are an attempt to further weaken the ANC. The DA, which is already governing the Western Cape Province, is determined to win at least two more provinces in the coming elections, and viewing their growth and campaigning strategies in the past years, one is tempted to say it is possible.

1

The Secret Minutes

Nelson Mandela was released from prison on 11 February 1990. We gathered that talks had already been going on between himself and his captors. We were also told that a number of important points had already been underscored. When P. W. Botha in his Rubicon speech told the nation that Nelson Mandela did not want to come out of prison, he insisted on saying that Mandela had arrested himself. As the National Party, they were prepared to release him on the condition that he renounces violence. Nelson Mandela had responded by pointing out that he had not arrested himself and that the captive could not negotiate his release; as an incarcerated prisoner, he could only be released by those who had captured him.

We gathered that Mandela was already negotiating with his captors at Victor Verster Prison and was being treated differently from the other Rivonia trialists. Well, whatever the case, that is not the issue at this juncture. There were minutes discussed before the formation of the constituent assembly called the Convention for a Democratic South Africa (CODESA). In these minutes, their contents are not clearly elucidated, and their secrecy cannot be revealed for public consumption. Their very nature of being secret entails that they won't be available for public scrutiny; otherwise, they will lose their being secret.

A number of things emerged, and amongst others were the transfer of power from the racist regime to the government of the people, the land question, the safeguarding of the Western imperialists' capital, and education, which had been kept inferior for black people. In fact, it was a discussion on how to keep the systems going. The fear of the white minority was based on a mistrust of the black government. Most of the African countries which had been decolonised remained under Third World conditions.

The Groote Schuur Minute, which discussed the talks about talks, began to look at the ways of levelling the playing field for the talks to resume. In these talks about talks, a number of points emerged. One of the arguments from the pan-Africanist school of thought was that the enemy was negotiating from a position of strength because he had not been defeated militarily—the enemy camp represented by the National Party was still waging a war against African people, the state of emergency was still in place, and the assassins, mercenaries, and homeland vigilantes were still at large. The National Party had unleashed the dogs of war on all angles. This terrible scenario was unhealthy for the talks to commence.

The playing field was not levelled. The enemy was strong, and therefore, he was going to dictate the terms on how South Africa would be governed in the future. The ANC had emerged as the strongest negotiator, and it became apparent that they had conquered the moral high ground. They owned the process partly because strong figures like Nelson Mandela, Walter Sisulu, Govan Mbeki, and others were highly recognised by the international community.

The most important element of the discussion was the Western imperialists' capital. The countries of the West have investments in South Africa, and whatever form and shape the discussions were going to take, they had to carry with them the confidence of the Western capitalists. Before the release of Nelson Mandela, the white business community and the Afrikaner academics led by Dr Frederik van Zyl Slabbert had already started the journey to Dakar in Senegal, which meant that before CODESA in Kempton Park, the talks were already underway. CODESA was just a façade meant to show the world that there were serious discussions taking place even though the future of South Africa had long been concluded in the secret minutes. All other parties were just rubber-stamping what had been concluded at the venues of the secret meetings.

2

The Unbanning of the Liberation Movements

South Africans fought for their freedom; they fought and liberated themselves from the shackles of bondage and racial discrimination. In 1983 the National Party introduced the tricameral parliament, a parliament that left black people outside the legislative assembly. By forming the tricameral parliament, the National Party was groping in the dark, digging its own grave. Little did they know that their action would result in a rolling mass action which would coerce them to abandon the reins of power.

The tricameral parliament was made up of three houses, which were represented by the whites, Indians, and coloureds. The House of Delegates (HOD) represented the Indian community, while the House of Representatives (HOR) represented the coloured community. Black people of African origin had no place in this parliamentary set-up; they were ostracised on the grounds that they had their tribal homelands. The homelands were also called Bantustans; these were the places where Africans could practise their self-determination, as P. W. Botha would insist.

The people of South Africa who had not gone to exile and those who were not in prison came together on 20 August 1983 in Cape Town under the umbrella body of the United Democratic Front (UDF). They gathered to contribute to the last push for the total eradication of the evil system of apartheid. These South Africans came from all walks of life. The UDF was composed of the civil structures of communities, such as women's movements, civic organisations, football associations, community organisations, church movements, youth organisations, student movements, burial societies, workers and the unemployed, and the physically challenged amongst others. These South Africans were led by a very gifted and brave cleric by the name of Allan Boesak, the Durban attorney and the political activist Mr Archie Gumede, and Mrs Albertina Sisulu, the wife of the late Robben Island prisoner Mr Walter Sisulu.

It was under the courageous leadership of these stalwarts that the people of South Africa began to organise their communities: the rent boycotts in the Vaal Triangle under the national organiser of the UDF Mr Patrick 'Terror' Lekota; the consumer boycotts; the bus boycotts in the Eastern Cape, Soweto, Kathorus, and Mamelodi next to Pretoria; the strikes and national stay-away under a strong leadership of the Congress of South African Trade Unions (COSATU), a trade union federation; and other related formations. Activities were all over the country, with the militancy of the youth in townships taking the lead in confronting the South African Defence Force (SADF), the deadly force of the heretical regime. Street committees and kangaroo courts were formed with the aim of undermining the apartheid courts and their laws. The youth was very instrumental in the efforts to effect changes. Through their military action and their activities, which undermined the apartheid government, they rendered the country ungovernable.

The National Party admitted that it was becoming humanly impossible to defend apartheid and that there was a need for an open dialogue with the ANC and other banned organisations. The economy was taking a nosedive, the centre could not hold, and it became extremely hard to continue to defend the illegitimate system, which had also been declared by the United Nations as crime against humanity. There was a simmer of a massive upsurge, and the country was teetering on the brink of the abyss. The unstable environment became hostile to the racist regime that had been riding roughshod over the black masses.

This scenario paints a bleak picture of the South African past, and it disputes a number of theories regarding the freedom of our country. There are people who claim to have liberated South Africa even though they were not in the scene of the war. It was the people's camp versus the enemy's camp, and both of them were composed of all races in the country. The UDF adopted the Freedom Charter; the document had been written and adopted by the Congress of the People in Kliptown in 1955, which also became the core document of the ANC. The UDF further demanded the release of Nelson Mandela and his comrades from Robben Island and all other political prisoners in the country. For the creation of a conducive climate on which the talks could commence, the UDF exerted more pressure on the South African government by demanding the withdrawal of troops from the townships, the return of all exiles, and the commencement of talks about the future of the country. A number of demands were made, and all of them were made by the people who had not gone to exile.

Amongst the people's demands were the unbanning of political organisations, such as the PAC, ANC, Communist Party, and others. It is a fallacy that the UDF was a springboard of any of the organisations counted above. It is also untrue that a particular voice from exile had been given to the 'inxiles' to liberate themselves, albeit the struggle of the ANC at this time was guided by four pillars—campaigning for the international isolation of South Africa, mass mobilisation, establishing underground structures in environments where they were banned, and the guerrilla warfare in the arms struggle.

South Africans took their own initiatives and assessed the strengths and weaknesses of the government of the day. They formed their own street committees and undermined the collaborating councillors and the institutions of the ruling National Party. A person who was in exile, it should be noted, was in the trenches of the struggle outside the country. Not all of them were fighting the just wars for liberation; some of them were in the best universities of the world, enjoying academic freedom, which had been deprived to those who were fighting the enemy from the inside. The ANC's mission in exile assisted a lot in highlighting the plight of black South Africans; it gave awareness to the international community by accentuating the outcry of the people inside the country. This process was able to reverberate the lamentation of the toiling masses. The underground activities and the military incursions through the guerrilla warfare and similar tactics were reinforced by the strength and resilience of the people inside the country.

It should also be noted that some fence-sitters and those who are now reaping the fruits of our freedom were either claiming to be neutral or were working with the enemy as agents provocateurs and informers. Some of them were identified and driven away from the townships, and in retaliation, others formed the vigilante groups and smaller units to retaliate. Others came out in the open and allowed themselves to be used by the National Party, and they openly defended white supremacy.

The struggle to liberate the oppressed in South Africa was fought by the South Africans themselves, and they liberated themselves; this point should be reiterated. The people of South Africa witnessed the coming down of a powerful government which was armed to teeth. The apartheid government was butchering children in the townships, but the dastardly acts of the apartheid regime were condemned all over the world, and the isolation of the National Party government forced them to bow to the pressures and start negotiations.

It is very painful today to notice that the ANC has isolated people who were in the forefront of our struggle, such as Rev. Allan Boesak and a number of other township activists. Firebrands who were able to catch the bull by its horns have now been sidelined to the periphery, and activists who fought fearlessly when they were only armed with the Molotov cocktails (petrol bomb) and stones are now left with broken hearts in the townships. These fire-eaters were so brave that they confronted an army which was armed more than any other army in the African continent.

The Afrikaners had boasted that they could walk over the entire African continent and wipe out any form of resistance in their way. This mighty army was frustrated by the strategies, resilience, relentless vigour, and determination of the people and the young comrades in the townships; in short, it was a people's war. All strategies for guerrilla warfare for the combatants were practised by young schoolboys who were commanded in the townships; it was motivated by the spirit of no surrender and the undying love for their country and the thirst for freedom.

Activists know one another, and no one can confuse people about their legitimate leaders. The opportunists have begun to tell lies and claim easy victories, but no one can claim to have been in the forefront when South Africans were facing the full might of the evil army. Children were sent to prison when P. W. Botha declared the state of emergency in 1985.

I was detained on July 1986. The special branch came in and picked me up from the school where I was doing my practice as a teacher in the making. I was accused of instigating youths to engage in acts of violence. I was also asked about my role in student politics. I was condemned for fighting against gutter education, which was designed by the white racist regime to be fed to black people and force them to accept their inferiority. In 1987 I was elected the chairperson of the South African National Student Congress (SANSCO) at Umbumbulu College of Education.

In June 1987 I was detained again, and I was interrogated in the Pinetown Police Station. The special branch accused me of inciting violence against the members of the Inkatha Freedom Party in Clermont. I protested that I was a student studying far away from home and that I was at a boarding school. I asked them to get their facts straight because the lousy detentions were not helping them either—whichever informant fabricating lies about me was misleading them—and that they should check their facts before they detain people.

SANSCO at this time was led by Billy Ramokgopa, who is now a medical doctor; he had done his last year in the medical school at the University of Natal (the Steve Biko campus). It was in this year (1987) that we attended a conference in Cape Town, the Peninsula Technikon (Pentech), where I met the youth firebrand Peter Mokaba for the first time. The words of welcome had been delivered to us by Prof. Jakes Gerwel, who later served in the office of President Nelson Mandela as a spin doctor. The conference elected Bongani More, who replaced the outgoing Billy Ramokgopa.

Our student life was vibrant; we were active in our campuses regardless of the brutal repression exerted on us by the then minister of education, Mr F. W. de Klerk. At this time, de Klerk was pushing a bill in parliament which was going to forbid all forms of protests and ban the activities of student organisations, such as SANSCO. Some few white students came to our conference to pledge their solidarity, and they also requested us to support them in their concerted efforts to end conscription of the only white teenagers to the South African Defence Force (SADF). Most of us were detained during this time.

The United Nations and the international community persuaded P. W. Botha to release children because of their age and that most of them were students. Besides the pressure from the outside, we also engaged in hunger strikes where most of us were able to draw international attention and sympathies. These were the struggles as they were told by us who did not fold our hands when fate demanded us to defend ourselves and the dignity of our people.

August 2013 marked the thirtieth anniversary of the formation of the United Democratic Front (UDF), and nothing was ever heard from the ANC; three decades of our struggle were ignored and trivialised. This is a very sad scenario in the history of our country.

The unbanning of the liberation movements came in with a lot of confusion, especially to those who had been in the trenches of the struggle inside the country. The PAC returned from exile and started their political activities but failed to get into the grass roots and mobilise their membership. The focus of the struggle had been on the ANC and the release of the Robben Island prisoners, especially Nelson Mandela. The leaders of the PAC who had been incarcerated with Nelson Mandela did not receive the same reception as those of ANC. When the election fever gained momentum, the PAC could not mobilise their rank and file convincingly. Instead, many petty squabbles emerged amongst the leadership, and as a result, they did not perform very well in the 1994 first democratic election. Their camp was chaotic.

The military wing of the PAC (Poqo) was not as popular as ANC's Umkhonto we Sizwe. The integration of the armed forces was initiated by the ANC and the National Party; therefore, Poqo had to be swallowed by SANDF, and it had to bow to the commands and dictates of ANC's military commissars. The South Africans were robbed of the pan-Africanist ideology, and ANC's negotiated settlement gained dominance. When the results were announced after the election, the PAC became a 1 per cent party. From there onwards, there was nothing positive about the PAC, and all that we could hear about were the fights and factionalism within. Many newly formed parties, such as UDM of General Bantu Holomisa and COPE of Terror Lekota and Mbhazima 'Sam' Shilowa, were able to win the hearts and minds of many people than that of the PAC despite its long record of the struggle.

If a liberation movement fails to define itself to the masses, it loses support, and the limelight is stolen by those who are popularised by the international community and the powers that be of the Western world. The PAC is like dead wood; it exists only in name, and there is no hope that it can still make a comeback. The recently formed Economic Freedom Fighters (EFF) of Julius Malema has made a mark in parliament, and in the South African political discourse, this has further rubbed more salt in the wound of the PAC. In fact, it has overtaken many.

The PAC is like a defunct organisation whose offices are unknown to the masses. They can no longer claim any victory from their glorious movement, and their history can only be told by their rival in the struggle, the ANC. The ANC can tell the stories in their own way, and they can discredit them as they wish. In fact, they used to do that in the sixties; it was reflected in Mandela's Rivonia Trial speech, where he says he will fight white domination and black domination alike, meaning the black dominance accentuated in the slogan of the PAC (Africa belongs to Africans).

The unbanning of the liberation movements came with a number of other problems. Take the ANC, for instance; the establishment of the offices inside the country was not a walk in the park what with the infiltration of the National Party spies and the joining of the reactionary elements, some of whom had been attracted by the gravy train which came with the new dispensation and wealth that the ANC was about to inherit.

Most of the MK soldiers felt that they had been abandoned without any income and were just thrown into the wild and told to go and fend for themselves. The military integration process took a long time, and because of idleness and the lack of income, most of these cadres began to get into activities of crime, robberies, and petty theft. The usage of the AK-47 rifles in heist operations became common; the guns that were meant to liberate the country began to terrorise citizens and business people in particular.

Some of the soldiers of liberation became disillusioned. A recent incident involved the leader of the MK veterans Mr Kebby Maphatsoe, who uttered out statements that are putting the ANC into disrepute; all these bear testimony to the existing disgruntlement of the ANC cadres. Mr Maphatsoe claimed to have been in the ANC camps in Uganda, where he was shot by the Ugandan forces in the arm when he tried to escape. His arm was amputated; he thinks that this gives him licence to bully other people around. Before the ANC made him deputy minister of defence, he had insulted other members of the MK veterans who were dissatisfied about the way ANC governed the country. He told them to go to hell, and when they questioned his credentials, he told them that they were not members of MK in the first place. They began to slander his character, casting aspersions on and questioning his credentials until it was later discovered that the long-mouthed buffoon had only been a cook in the Ugandan camps of the MK and that he had acted like a dissident when he tried to run away from the very same MK camps. These cadres later formed the organisation called South Africa First, and they voiced out their discontent about Kebby Maphatsoe's style of leadership.

In one of the meetings where Maphatsoe was addressing the veterans and the ANC members, he ended up diverting from the subject at hand and spoke about Ms Thuli Madonsela, the public protector. Ms Madonsela had given a directive that Zuma should pay the money that was used in his house for non-security features; he had to pay a portion of the 246 million rand, which it is claimed was used for the security reasons. Ms Madonsela has ordered that Zuma pay all the money that was used in every non-security feature. But Mr Maphatsoe says no, that Zuma should not pay that money, and he further went on to call Madonsela a CIA spy. When Thuli Madonsela asked him to come up with evidence, he began to flounder around, trying to deny that he had uttered such words. When the journalists came up with recorded evidence, Maphatsoe waffled like a guilty child trying to explain himself. Madonsela asked him to retract his statement and apologise sincerely or face the might of the law; he reluctantly apologised, and he was embarrassed all over the world.

Who appointed this idiot? A DA member of parliament had to leave the chambers after failing to withdraw the words he had used; he had called Maphatsoe an idiot. The USA came with guns blazing, asking the South African government to explain if this buffoon represented the opinion of the SA government or if he had just been smoking some stupefying weeds. The ANC and the government distanced themselves from this comedian and his sense of humour. This is a true reflection of the type of leaders we have nowadays. Any clown can be a leader as long as he sings the praises of the ANC's elite. The issue of selecting good leaders with talent remains a thorny subject as we tolerate mediocrity, incompetence, corruption, and all sorts of immoral behaviour in our government leaders.

In 1991 Maphatsoe and other cadres decided to escape from the ANC camps in Uganda. He had not been serving in the forefront of Umkhonto we Sizwe; he was just a cook in the kitchens of the camp. He claims that he was running away because the situation in the camps was intolerable and that he therefore had to escape and report to the leadership inside South Africa. This cook has failed to tell us that he wanted to come back because positive changes had occurred.

Nelson Mandela was already out of prison, and many exciting things were happening inside the country. Ill-disciplined people like Maphatsoe were on the rush to get inside the country and claim the accolades even if their actions were ignoring protocol. Why would a disciplined soldier fail to tolerate the exile conditions when he was just serving in the kitchen? They were not starving. Conditions were not as bad as he exaggerates them. He was shot by the Ugandan armed forces while trying to escape. He had to be amputated.

The unbanning of the liberation movements brought a lot of hope into our country and the world, but today many activists are puzzled by what is going on in the new government, the type of leaders, and their questionable moral standards.

3

Reality for the 'Inxiles'

Amongst the demands of the people's camp inside the country were the release of Nelson Mandela and all political prisoners, the unbanning of all political organisations and their free participation in the discussion of a new political dispensation, the soldiers of the South African Defence Force (SADF) had to be removed from the Frontline States and the townships in order to commence the talks, a conducive climate had to be created. The international community had applied sanctions, and the National Party was feeling isolated from world politics.

The South Africans wanted to participate in international sports. The Springboks were missed by the entire world in rugby, the Proteas were unable to take part in the international cricket tournaments, the South African athletes could not participate in the Olympics, and people like Zola Budd experienced the South African boycott campaigns by the international sports community; they were ostracised all over. A lot of good talent was suppressed by the unnecessary sustenance of apartheid.

The Springboks proved that they were indeed missed; their first appearance in the World Cup of 1995 gave a conclusive proof that they were the world champions. They convincingly won the Webb Ellis Cup at the Ellis Park Stadium. The South African soccer squad won the CAF Cup in 1996.

When President F. W. de Klerk announced the release of Nelson Mandela and that all bans were rescinded, there was jubilation all over the world. The inxiles were even more jubilant than anyone else because they were the ones who were feeling the heat. The happiness was written in their eyes, in the air, and elsewhere; new hopes of peace and prosperity were revived as they witnessed Mandela walking free out of Victor Verster Prison. The moment of truth had finally arrived. The ANC returned from exile, and the preparations for the talks began.

The agenda on the talks was unknown, and it took a lot of time for the terms of reference to be concluded. It is during this period of patient waiting that the reality of the situation emerged. Despite the brutal killing of the people in Boipatong and other townships, the inxiles were dumbfounded as they observed their internal leadership, especially that of the UDF, being sidelined. Allan Boesak, the national president of the UDF, was not included in the talks. Instead, after a couple of years, he was imprisoned for theft and corruption under the new government of the ANC. It still leaves us confused and mind-boggled as we try to figure out the reason why such a powerful cleric would be recalled from his lecturing post in the US and be tried in South African courts, using the old apartheid laws, and ultimately be found guilty of sins committed under the critical times of freedom fighting. This was the reality for the inxiles, a wake-up call.

Oscar Mpetha, one of the firebrands of the people's war and a highly respected unionist, was not there when the talks began. Nothing was ever heard again about this UDF stalwart. We gathered that in his birthday in 1992, he received one card from an unknown comrade wishing him a happy birthday. He died of stroke, and no one could confirm the day of his death; he was not given a state funeral.

As for Winnie Madikizela-Mandela, it is hard to know where to start when you try to talk about the suffering of this woman. Authors can produce volumes of books when they write about Winnie, but to be specific and relevant to this topic, Winnie Madikela-Mandela was swamped with a multitude of charges and was nearly sentenced to prison. You don't need to be a genius to read the writings on the wall; even an imbecile can see. Winnie had become too powerful for what the ANC needed from her; she was enjoying too much power, and somehow her wings had to be curtailed and pruned to size. The inxiles rated Winnie exceedingly higher compared to the leaders from exile.

She was the mother of the nation. Wherever her people were suffering, she was the first to be there and give her sincerest consolation. The enemy hated her; the people loved her such that she was perceived by the leaders from exile as becoming bigger than the ANC and a very serious threat. Some of her utterances, which under normal circumstances would have been treated lightly, were blown out of proportion by the people who were supposed to protect her. Instead of enjoying the process leading to the freedom of her people, she was in and out of courts and, on some instances, on the verge of a prison gate.

As for Mzwakhe Mbuli, the People's Poet, this is another powerful individual who landed himself into trouble. His skill of writing poetry never failed to arouse many people's admiration. Mzwakhe was able to incite and instigate the people to action when they were in situations of doubt and despair. When they lost all hope as activists, Mzwakhe with his baritone voice would revive them back to action. When they were running out of steam and losing strength, his commanding voice would be heard saying, 'A new man is born full of strength and agility, to demonstrate conventional wisdom in defence of the fatherland, through cannons of criticism his dragon force and enthusiasm shall perform a daring combat against Fascism.' Their spirits would be revived and lifted up by these words, and they would be rejuvenated to confront the enemy again.

What happened to this gentleman? Mzwakhe was an altruistic person, and just like Winnie Mandela, he was loved by many people on the ground. He had been to Pietermaritzburg, where he contributed a lot of his own money to the victims of floods which were the results of a hurricane. A few months after this good deed, Mzwakhe Mbuli was arrested. We were all taken aback. After making a contribution of over 40,000 rand to the flood victims, Mzwakhe was 'caught red-handed' after a robbery at the FNB (one of South Africa's biggest banks). This was disturbing news, and no one wanted to believe this except his prosecutors. We were told he was caught with 15,000 rand in his possession.

It's all confusing isn't it? One minute you are this good benefactor contributing 40,000, and before sunset, you go to the bank to rob 15,000 rand. Something doesn't add up here; even the dumbest of all dunderheads would be able to do the addition. He was sentenced to years in prison until former leader of the opposition Mrs Helen Suzman was touched and stood up to confront this blatant infringement of justice. She successfully convinced the parole board to consider the matter as a manipulation of justice, and Mzwakhe was released.

The inxiles were left shocked and struggling to figure out who will be the next, and while we were still asking ourselves so many questions, another stalwart of the UDF died. Mr Archie Gumede's death opened a vacuum on the leadership of altruistic people; he was not given a state funeral. This humble giant had fought fiercely in the seventies when he launched a release Mandela campaign, and he became the Natal president of the UDF and was always on the side of the masses whenever they were at their lowest ebb. And because he was an attorney, he represented poor people without charging them anything. You would see him walking in the streets of Pinetown without any bodyguard, and in the afternoon, he would take a bus to Clermont and travel with common people, using a public transport. He was a true leader of the people who exhausted all his family resources for the people of SA to be free. Archie Gumede was a true patriot.

And I am talking about a man who was my mentor. I was honoured to have rubbed shoulders with this stalwart since the age of fourteen. He was a true combatant, not the type of leader who would be compared to the politicians that we see today. I am talking about a selfless individual who dedicated his life to the struggle of his people; he was the son of Josiah Gumede, former president of the African National Congress (ANC).

What happened to this humble giant? Regardless of the fact that he was a member of parliament and that he had served the UDF for so many years when the ANC was banned, most of the top leadership of the ANC were visibly absent in his funeral. He received the funeral of a commoner, which was not given coverage on the national television; it was reported for a few seconds or less than a minute.

I visited him at St Aidan's Hospital when he was on the verge of a grave yard. He told me that he had requested to see Nelson Mandela, but Mandela had blatantly refused to have a meeting and had told him to follow the protocol by starting at branch level. He was very upset and disappointed with this arrogance. The inxiles were left confused while trying to put together some pieces of this confusing jigsaw puzzle. The world had forgotten about Archie Gumede and his role. Most of us are victimised by the ANC because we are considered as his products.

All that followed this was hearing about leaders being caught up in a web of embezzlement, corruption, and self-aggrandisement. The ruling elite have turned into self-enriching thieves. Our people have no one to listen to their cries, and their plight is worse than before. UDF leaders in our townships are either sidelined or labelled as being double agents and agents provocateurs. Good brains are being jettisoned, and we witness our townships going back to the state of violence and crime.

Councillors who were never seen anywhere during the times of struggle are now empowering themselves at the expense of the suffering masses. Some of these uneducated scoundrels, who can neither read nor write a document, are serving in the EXCOs of metro municipalities, the highest decision-making bodies of the land.

They waffle and flounder while struggling to explain themselves in the chambers to the joyous laughter of the opposition, and the ANC appears to be content with this type of arrangement. Just visit the municipalities in any part of the country and see how embarrassing they can be as they become dinner for the DA.

As I write this piece of work right now, the councillors of the ANC have given their mayor in the Tlokwe Municipality a vote of no confidence. They voted with the DA, and he has since been removed from office and replaced with a DA candidate. Look and observe them as they walk in the corridors of power, confused and powerless. The people on the ground are beginning to lose patience, and as the ANC keeps on talking about the unfinished revolution, they must brace themselves for a different type of revolution.

The simmering discontent of the masses is likely to have a turnabout; the petitions submitted every day to the mayors and government officials are about to spark a massive upsurge which no leader of the ANC will be able to contain. A true revolution is fermenting, and it won't be televised.

4

The Persistence of Racism

Racism remains a plague and a thorny issue in South Africa. We are talking about the racial stereotypes, hypocrisy, disproportionate allocation of resources, prioritisation, skills to access better jobs, privileges in education and elsewhere, residential areas, legacies of the past, and land question. In fact, institutionalised racism is still very much with us.

A certain section of the white people is always complaining about the economy taking a nosedive under the predominantly black government. They are always whining about corruption and nothing good in the African government. While I cannot dispute this theory, we should remember that changes do not happen overnight.

The economy, for instance, is entirely controlled by the whites. They are still enjoying the privileges that they had under the apartheid regime. The whole manufacturing sector still remains in the hands of the whites and maybe a bit to the Indians. If you were to visit the Johannesburg Stock Exchange, everything that goes on there will give you enough evidence of who is in charge of the economy in this country.

South Africa is highly industrialised. There is no country in the entire African continent that can claim to match the South African economy, and yet the ownership of that industry belongs to one race—the whites. The top jobs in management and administration still remain reserved for the whites. The ruling elite do not come up with the policies that seek to redress this imbalance. There are no concrete equity policies in the ANC agenda to correct the wrongs of the past.

Since 1994 the ANC has come up with the Reconstruction and Development Program (RDP), which was abandoned in the space without redressing the legacy of the past and inequality. As a result, black people are still providing cheap labour to the holders of the means of production, who happen to be white. Another economic policy, the GEAR, came out during the tenure of President

Thabo Mbeki, Zumas's predecessor, but it was vehemently opposed by the trade unions under the federation COSATU (the alliance partner), and the former finance minister was entrusted with the task of coming up with a new policy. He had tabled the NDP, which had received a negative reception from the leftists of the ANC itself and the radical elements within COSATU. This NDP was applauded by the whites as one of the best policies. The details and the economic analysis of the NDP will be given later in the following chapters.

The black workers are still toiling as they used to do. What is more surprising is the arrogance that is still demonstrated by the white bosses. Under the presidency of Nelson Mandela, they continued to unfairly retrench the workers, telling them to go to Mandela. The white community protested about everything that was done by the government despite the fact that many ministers were white. The ANC government elevated the women to top positions, such as cabinet ministers, something which was unheard of under the apartheid government. White women themselves have benefitted from this new dispensation. They were not as many as we see them now in parliament and in the provincial legislatures. They are MECs, and in the municipalities, they are councillors. It is surprising to note that they are whining about every little mistake that is done by a predominantly black government despite the fact that the ANC has not excluded them in governance. They continue to shed crocodile tears regardless of the fact that they still hold 82 per cent of the land.

In his book *The Pedagogy of the Oppressed*, Paulo Freire argues that if an oppressor frees the oppressed, the freedom that is enjoyed by his former slave becomes oppression to the master. This happens because he can no longer give commands. If his requests are tantamount to commands, he is quickly called to order by the person that for a number of years he had regarded as his inferior. Little privileges that black people enjoy in the new South Africa are very irritating to a person with a mentality of an oppressor and a racist.

It annoys white people to see a liberated black person. This is noticeable in the shops, on the roads when they rudely blow their horns at a slightest mistake done by a black person, the services that they give to black people, and the continued insult of calling them baboons, monkeys, and Kaffirs. On 10 May 1994 when Nelson Mandela delivered a speech, he had pointed out that no Indian shall ever be called a coolie and that no black person shall be called a Kaffir any more, and yet these words are still loosely used by the whites in shopping malls, in schools, and in farms. At face value, South Africa appears to be a united country, a rainbow nation, and a land of opportunities, but in reality, black people still bear the brunt of oppression and reformed apartheid. This is even tolerated by our children in the predominantly white schools as they are told that they are inferior to their white and Indian counterparts despite the fact that some of them are excelling in mathematics and science.

Institutionalised racism still affects the residential areas and the disproportionate allocation of resources. Chatsworth, the nearest Indian township, to me is still an area for the Asians, and there has never been a serious effort to integrate black people and other races there. Wentworth and Bluff are areas for coloured people, who are also whining about the deprivation of opportunities. They are protesting about their level of melanin—under the apartheid government, they were not white enough, and under the new dispensation, they are not black enough. The people of KwaMashu and Umlazi are African. They are complaining about the shortage of resources in their townships compared to the neighbouring residential areas of other races. There are shopping malls in these townships, but all the shops are owned by the whites and a bit by the Indians. Black people are not given economic opportunities in their own townships.

How does this happen in the country with a black president, a country that was liberated twenty years ago. How long will this continue? These are the questions asked by black people as they observe the country which is in the South of Africa. Durban is the largest port in the African continent and is one of the biggest cities in the sub-Saharan Africa, but the CBD of this city is dominated by other races. Black people, especially the Zulus, who happen to be the majority in KZN, have no properties and no shops in this area. You can criss-cross the whole town, but there is no business for the Zulu people in this town. They only come as shoppers, give the money to other races, withdraw back to their poor places, and mourn while foreign races are counting their profits and laughing all the way to the bank. This is the persistence of racism and segregation in South Africa under the government of the ANC.

In his book *South Africa's Brave New World*, R. W. Johnson talks about failed colonisation. He equates the ANC to all liberation movements in the African continent. In his gloomy outlook, he points out, 'Yet it seems likely that the ANC will be in power for years to come. The result is continuing slide in standards backwards from the levels set in the days of white rule, posing the worrying question of where the slide will stop.'

I dispute what Johnson is saying. It's a slide in standard, but the question is, for whom? Black people, who have always been at the bottom of the pile, are experiencing no slide. They have remained where the apartheid avalanche left them; it's only that they have been joined by some races who had better privileges at the top under the white rule.

Johnson says, 'South Africa is emphatically different, its economy incomparably more sophisticated, various and developed. It is a country of six-lane highways, computers and jet planes.' When the Gauteng community complained about the e-tolls (the revamped Gauteng roads where the residents are required to foot the bill by paying for the tolls), President Jacob Zuma told them that the South African roadways were different from those of countries like Malawi, and President Joyce Banda of Malawi took exception to this arrogance. We know that South Africa has advanced roadways which are comparable to those in Europe, and we appreciate that our country has that sophistication. They were built by the advanced engineering of white men and the sweat, toil, and exploitation of cheap black labour.

All streets in the white suburbs are tarred, while township roads are either full of potholes—which means that when they were built, standards were ignored—or remain gravel roads. While I agree with Johnson and Zuma on the point of six-lane highways and perhaps their improvements, I argue that this sophistication should be on par with the growth of all citizens so that the wealth and beauty of our country will be enjoyable to the majority of people, if not all. I also need to stress that computers and jet planes mean nothing to a poor black person, who still languishes in the slums of old South Africa. The sophisticated economy does not benefit the masses of our people, who remain unemployed in the townships.

On education, Johnson talks about 'affirmation' (that is, discrimination) in admissions and appointment policies which are bound to lower standards more and more over time. For example, the University of Cape Town medical school—once the best in the country—admits black and coloured students who gained three Bs and three Cs in their school leaving exam, whereas five As and a B are required to admit a white or Indian student. All this does is to encourage emigration of talented whites or Indians and to ultimately produce black and coloured doctors with substandard reputation.

Once more Mr Johnson fails to understand that black people never received education; the little that was given to them was called Bantu education. This gutter education never taught anything to black people except to be subservient and to get the basic understanding of a few terminologies so as to make it easier to communicate with a white boss. It was geared towards the needs of slavery and servitude, the inferior and superior kind of relationship between the black and white peoples. Mr Johnson here appears to be a victim of ignorance and a wrong racist upbringing because when you read the whole book, you discover that there is not even a single instance where he speaks about black talent or anything good about his fellow black countrymen.

Black people are human beings. They fall in love just like all other human beings in the world. They appreciate beauty. They would like to show affection to their wives and children in public. They have manners and respect, which were not taught at school since a white man wanted to make them look uncouth and uncivilised. Bantu education never taught all these things, and no one can talk about Bantu education except the victims of this well-designed evil. When you see a black man failing to open the door for his wife, blame it on his education. When a black woman shouts to the person next to her when she is supposed to be soft-spoken, don't accuse her of being uncouth; blame it on her education. When black people go around eating things and throwing rubbish on the streets and littering, blame it on their education, and hopefully you will understand the damage that was done by inferior and gutter education that had been designed by a white man for a specific purpose. White people do not understand the damage that was done by inferior education to black people, the damage which the ANC has no intention of correcting because it will raise false hopes and will make black people think that they are equal to the whites. All what you see is the damage which was well researched by Hendrik Verwoerd. Today white people are reaping the fruits that were planted by the apartheid architects.

If black people appear to be foolish, please forgive them; they are the victims of years and years of deprivation. This trend is still going to continue for quite some time because the ANC, as it has been pointed out before, serves the interests of the whites. They have no programme for rectifying the damage. They are safeguarding the monopoly of Western capital, and before they took over from their National Party friends, they had a number of secret meetings where, amongst other things, the National Party advised them that if they want to govern in peace, they must keep the standard of black men's education lower than Bantu education—in other words, 'Make it lower than what we've been offering them.' Educated people are clever. They ask too many questions. It is easy to govern an illiterate nation. This is what is presently happening in our country as far as education is concerned. It's not a mistake; it's by design.

The symbols used to pass and fail students at their school leaving classes are not the time criterion by which to judge the intrinsic worth of black and coloured students, Mr Johnson. The conditions under which those students acquired those symbols are horrible. I even appreciate that they are able to get the exemptions because some of them are born in squatter camps, others in extreme conditions of abject poverty, and others in the conditions of slums, which are similar to those in Europe in the Middle Ages. Before we blow trumpets, we must empathise with the black people's conditions and lifestyle.

On the part of African nationalism, Mr Johnson makes a comparison between the Anglo and the Boer nationalism, and he compares these thus, placing the dichotomy above African nationalism. Again African people are supposed to take over the reins of power and begin the process of rectifying the mistakes of their colonisers. In the case of South Africa, the foreigners came to the South African borders and began to fight their own European wars in the Anglo–Boer War. African people observed this. When the foreigners were through, they began to divide the country and shared the power. When the British decided to withdraw, they gave power to the Boers and asked them to continue to do their dirty work on African people; they even left symbols such as the Union Jack on the old flag of South Africa. The mines continued to generate profits for the British and the Boers. Recently, as we speak, thirty-four African miners in Marikana were gunned down by the ANC government, and Lonmin, which is a British company, was at the forefront. Anglo American, Amplats, De Beers, etc.—all of them have been exploiting the mineral wealth of this country against the will of the indigenous people of the land.

The Boers took over the land at the barrel of a gun. African resistance met European military might. When the ANC took over, the land was still in the hands of the whites—it still is. Whatever form of African nationalism we think of, it will not work if African people are not in charge of the land. This theory goes a long way because it also affects the way we think. It affects elements of patriotism. It is easy for the Springboks to win as South Africans compared to Bafana Bafana. The Springboks are playing for their country, while the Bafana Bafana are playing as second citizens. Patriotism is just not there because they don't play for their country; they have no killer instincts compared to their white counterparts. African people are landless, and therefore, making a comparison between them and the Anglo–Boer alliance and British jingoism won't do justice to the topic at hand.

5

I Stand Accused Again

Racial stereotype, segregation, deprivation, lack of good education, colour bar, and discrimination are all vestiges of apartheid ideology that are still with us. This system deprived black majority the opportunities to grow, and it gave the white minority a number of privileges at the expense of black suffering. Even when the resources were in abundance, the insatiable appetite of white monopoly capital deprived black people entitlement to access them.

A shining example of this is that of a person who is prevented from entering a beachfront hotel because he happens to be black. He fights very hard for his freedom until he liberates himself from the discriminating system, only to discover that although he is free, he still cannot enter the hotel he had been barred from entering before. Colour bar signs, boom gates, and hurdles are gone, but he is still unable to enjoy the privileges he had been fighting for. The reason this time will be the way of gaining access to the hotel; it will be the income, the little money he earns compared to his white, Indian, or coloured counterparts. He is no longer discriminated because of the colour of his skin but by the entitlement determined by the scarcity of resources at his disposal. There is disproportionate allocation of resources, and the black leadership elevates the few elite and bar the rest from enjoying the fruits of freedom and the privileges which should have been provided by the changing times. Times have changed for the worst for this man.

The reality surfaces to this gentleman as he slowly accepts that the more things change, the more they appear to be looking the same. He learns that as he moves along with the vicissitudes of life, observing the oppressors changing faces, he has to learn to accept reality and that suffering is looking at him right in his face. He will grow in complacency. If he doesn't develop into a cynical, pessimistic critic that sees the gloomy side of everything, he will simply withdraw from public appearance and feel ashamed of himself. He will find solace in religion and preach to other comrades about the Second Coming of Jesus Christ, when all bad people will burn in hell (saying this while imagining his leaders) and all the good ones will be lifted up in a blink of an eye and enjoy everlasting love, peace, and prosperity. In heaven there'll be no sorrow, there will be no oppressors.

If he doesn't use religion as a new route to kingdom come, he becomes a soccer fanatic. He will choose to love his football team more than he loves his family. He is easily irritated by the slightest nagging from his wife. As he struggles with all the vagaries of life and the raw deal the entire situation is offering to him, he becomes short-tempered and hates everything that lives under the sun. He drives recklessly, and at the slightest provocation on the road, he engages into a silly fight and engages in road rage, not to mention if the other person happened to be of a different skin colour. He hallucinates at every mistake done by other people.

This is a lifestyle of a person who had high hopes when he fought for freedom, a person who finds it hard to accept the realities of a status quo, a person who never left a room for the disappointments he is now experiencing. It's worse if he was involved in the struggle for liberation but forgot to go to school. He has no academic qualifications, no apprenticeship, no certificate whatsoever, and life is extremely hard. All the promises made by the leaders when they were coming back from prisons and exile, all that the PAC promised—i.e. the return of the land of his forefathers and free education for his children. The years have gone by, and yet there is no socialist state. Instead, there is a raw deal of a welfare state, which encourages a daughter to get pregnant because she will be given a social grant, adding two unplanned grandchildren to his family's miseries.

While he struggles as the only breadwinner in this household called home, he continues to face uncertainties as strikes become the order of the day. He grew up under apartheid, where his father was always guaranteed a job. Even though there was terrible oppression, jobs were available on the abundance. There were no labour brokers, no strikes of this magnitude. As he reminisces on his own, he finally utters words in a soliloquy, and he quotes the words of the Israelites in the Sinai Desert, 'It was better in Egypt, at least we had food, water and shelter, look at where we are now, starving ourselves and our children in the desert.'

He thinks of his condition. In the last five years, he has lost two jobs, and he has been temporarily employed in three. He feels like shedding tears as he observes people who did not take part in the struggle for liberation enjoying the fruits of his toils. He remembers how he sang with passion freedom songs and slogans about heroes of the struggle who will come home and free him from the jaws of a lion, the discipline in the street committees where he participated, and how he followed orders of his commanders without question. Indeed, life is offering him a raw deal. Today all freedom songs and the struggle heroes are irritating him to the core; he feels nauseous at the mention of the names of the struggle's heroes.

After observing the hardships of life in Germany, Adolf Hitler refers to this gentleman using these words: 'And so this man, who was formerly so hard-working, grows lax in his whole view of life and gradually becomes the instrument of those who use him only for their own base advantage. He has so often been unemployed through no fault of his own that one time more or less ceases to matter, even when the aim is no longer to fight for economic rights, but to destroy political, social, or cultural values in general. He may not be exactly enthusiastic about strikes, but at any rate he has become indifferent' (*Mein Kampf*, 25).

6

The Land Question

The land was taken away at the barrel of a gun. African people were defeated and conquered. The superior military might of the Europeans overwhelmed African people. They were beaten hands down. If you are defeated, you become defenceless because your conqueror disarms you and forces you to listen to everything he says. All through the years, black people agonised and lamented as they observed the Europeans enjoying the fruits of their continent; they learnt to accept that their culture, values, norms, and everything else that they ever possessed had been taken away. The culture of dispossession still persists up to this moment.

They were forced to accept the Western ways of living and dress themselves like their new masters; they had to abandon their ways of worshiping and follow that of their conquerors. They had to think like Europeans, act like them, and even talk like them. The laws of dispossession taught them to abandon their ways of farming and go to the cities to look for work and adopt the new lifestyle that had been designed by the Westerners. Their cattle were reduced, and the discovery of mineral resources, such as gold and diamond, and the rapid industrialisation of countries like South Africa changed their lifestyle completely.

Education and religion brought forth with them a new kind of lifestyle that was completely different and foreign to theirs. The laws of racial segregation and discrimination, such as the Group Areas Act and the influx control laws, were introduced. African people found themselves being pushed into the peripheral reserves, most of which were rugged terrains with arid land and horrible conditions of soil texture. Some of them starved in these areas and found themselves being slowly coerced to migrate into the cities to provide cheap labour and be subjected to perpetual exploitation and modern slavery.

They were housed in hostels, township compounds, railway barracks, and four-roomed houses that looked like boxes of matches, and some of them were housed in filthy hostels which looked like houses of serfs in the Middle Ages, as observed by Senator Ted Kennedy of the USA in his visit in 1985 to witness the atrocities of apartheid. The lack of facilities in these reserves caused a lot of boredom, and criminal activities became the order of the day. Gangsterism and mafia styles were common as African criminals tried to imitate their American ghetto counterparts.

Land is essential, and it is a very strong component in redressing the legacies of the past. If government is determined to reverse poverty, land should be acquired whether by creating an environment where fair transactions of a willing buyer and a willing seller will prevail or through the means of expropriation. If either of the two is not realised, then we must brace ourselves for land-grabbing similar to that in Zimbabwe. People were not shy to rise up if they noticed that their leaders were playing games with their lives. The land-grab in Zimbabwe was not initiated by ZANU-PF; it was an uprising of the people on their own led by common people like Hitler Hunzvi, who was just a doctor. And that is not very far away from South Africa; it is looming on the horizon.

When white people divided the land, they chose the best arable areas, where they have gone on with commercial farming and made profits while being subsidised by their whites-only government. Even after twenty years of freedom, you find small and medium black farmers and a host of other rural peasants who farm for subsistence. There has been chaos in the programmes of land redistribution and restitution. This has happened because the ANC government is confused by everything. Because we have no good leadership, the programme of land restitution has been a dismal failure. Black people are given back their farms, but the government is anticipating them to fail.

AgriSA, one of the organisations of white farmers, has not been engaged with all their expertise to assist in training black farmers. The government has also failed to go in partnership with these boers so that when black people are given these farms, they are able to go commercial and compete equally on the importation and exportation of their food products. The yields of black farmers are lower than that of their white counterparts because of the shortage of skills and the failure of the government's agricultural departments to assist them in creating a good market for their products.

Some of the places taken away were not farms, but the government has failed black people as government ministers busily accuse black families who are failing to use the farms when in essence they were not commercial farmers when they were forcefully evicted by the white government. They have failed to build capacity so that those families will stop petty squabbles about inheritance and focus on farming—those who are interested anyway. Compensation must be given to those who are less interested to engage in farming activities. It is the duty of the government to maintain social order and to see to it that land is equally distributed amongst the members of these families and not to start programmes that are doomed to fail just to please white farmers and vindicate them that indeed black people are good for nothing.

The issue of land and its distribution remains a thorny issue; 83 per cent of South Africa's arable land is still occupied by the European minority. In former Bantustans or homelands, there are tracts of land which are used by a minority of black farmers; other portions remain fallow. In KZN there is vast land called Ingonyama Trust land, which is under the control of the king, and the vast portion of it is being underutilised. The farmers in these areas are unable to engage in commercial farming because the banks are not willing to give loans in the areas which have no title deeds. The farmers are given permission to occupy (PTOs), but without collateral, the banks are unable to fund the projects for farming in these areas.

7

Education and the Shortage of Skills

The National Party designed and orchestrated inferior education for black people. Dr Verwoerd had said it clearly that the natives had to be given the type of education that will keep them at their rightful place, that they needed no black mathematicians; he strongly felt that natives had to dream about the white men's lifestyle and see it as a utopia and a dream from afar. Black people had to serve their masters, as D. F. Malan had emphasised. When B. J. Voster came to power, he entrenched this system and took an extreme position of enforcing Afrikaans as the medium of communication and the only language used in conducting lessons in all South African schools. This action led to the school boycotts of 1976 (known as the Soweto uprisings), and a lot of blood was shed when the South African police opened fire on the unarmed African children.

A group of students led by a brave young man called Tsietsi Mashinini were vehemently opposed to the steps that had been designed to enforce Bantu education, which was regarded as gutter education meant to keep black students at a position inferior to their white counterparts. When the police started to open fire with live ammunition, the whole of Soweto was plunged into anarchy, and 600 young people were killed in cold blood. Hector Pieterson, a young boy of thirteen years, was shot dead; he became the symbol of this spate of violence and dastardly act waged by the South African police. The entire world condemned this brutal murder of innocent children, and 1976 became a turning point in the history of South Africa.

A question that rings succinctly into the minds of many is on the time when the ANC would correct the education backlog. How long are we going to wait for a better improvement of our education system? This simple question stems from the dithering policymakers and the implementation of their policies. From Bantu education, the OBE was introduced by Prof. Bhengu under the Mandela regime, and change is now being introduced. Both systems are not even understood by the people who are required to teach them. We have a government that lacks commitment, and education is not in their priority list. There are serious crises in our education. The basic education is poor from the first year up to the last class (matric), and higher education produces graduates who do not fit into the system. The South African education is in tatters with the lack of resources in African schools, as it used to be in the olden days of apartheid.

Policymakers are failing to design the type of education that is going to be geared to the needs of the country,

The predominantly white schools, or model Cs as they are known, are still reserved for the whites and the black middle class and the ruling elite. They are well resourced and expensive, while the African schools are under-resourced and overcrowded. Poor African children are denied access to the model Cs because of the exorbitant fees that are unaffordable to the parents of disadvantaged children. The lacking leadership in the ruling class is failing to address this perpetual inequality.

The ANC government closed down the teacher colleges and converted them to FET colleges; this happened in a country which was just emerging from years of oppression, when the teacher colleges had produced good teachers and the teaching profession had been noble. Poor black families were assisted by the young graduates from these colleges; they were producing breadwinners in African communities. When Jacob Zuma took over from Thabo Mbheki, he had promised to reopen these institutions; he is now approaching his last and second term in office, but not a single college has ever been opened. The overcrowding in classes is a testimony to the shortage of teachers, a crisis that was there in the previous apartheid government. The ANC government lacks commitment to redress these imbalances from the past.

Nursing colleges too were reduced in number; all professions that had been assisting black people in the past were either closed down or reduced. The police colleges, like the one in Hammanskraal, are no more.

There is still a shortage of books in schools, as what happened in our days.

The most embarrassing incident ever experienced by the present government was in the Limpopo Province,. The shortage of books in the schools was the result of the department's failure to deliver them on time or to deliver them at all. Mrs Angie Motshekga was left bruised and insulted by this saga. One would have expected the government that is led by black people to show more commitment, especially when it comes to education, but a dismal failure is noticeable.

White people have formed an organisation called Section 27, and they have exposed a number of mistakes in the Department of Education, including the textbook saga of Limpopo. In Limpopo the textbooks were supposed to be delivered to children at the beginning of the year, but by July, the books had not reached the intended recipients. In October they were found thrown in the river.

When Section 27 blew the whistle, the minister of education blamed the whites with a sinister agenda rather than openly admitting that things had gone wrong in her department. White people were merely concerned about the education of the children of their domestic workers, while SADTU, the South African Democratic Teachers Union, was siding with the ruling government.

There is chaos in the department; the left hand doesn't know what the right hand is doing. There is no proper planning. The teachers are not placed in their rightful positions, and there are white-elephant schools. At a recent case of schools in Port Elizabeth, the DDJ Jabavu in Motherwell was stripped by the locals brick by brick. Masangwana Primary School in New Brighton was looted to its foundations. The department had spent millions of rand in the construction of schools which were not needed by the community (*Sunday Times* of 16 November 2014). The ruins of Gqebera High School are still visible. The school had looked beautiful in September 2014, but the locals stripped it, and in October 2014, you could not tell where the school had been built. It had been stripped to its foundations. In Limpopo Province, schoolchildren are learning under the trees, but in the KZN Province, there are schools which are supposed to enrol 800 kids but have 250 only. Prioritisation in the Department of Education is nil. Thousands of teachers, including myself, are unemployed, and yet 2,000 posts for inspectors remain vacant.

There is a lack of security in schools. Students come to schools with dangerous weapons and stab one another to death in front of their teachers. Just like in the times of Bantu education, there are pupils who learn science until they complete their matric but without having used apparatuses. They cannot tell you what a test tube looks like. They haven't seen a laboratory in their lives—and this in a country which is richer than many countries in the developed world. Out of the 148 countries tested for mathematics, South Africa was rated number 147. Primary teachers for mathematics were given a Grade 6 paper to write, and 60 per cent of them failed. As to how an educator fails a paper that she is supposed to teach, it boggles the mind.

It becomes obvious that if education is not geared towards the needs of the country, there'll be shortage of skills and hence serious trouble for the country. The government of the day subsidises brain drain. Doctors of South Africa, especially the white students, are trained in medical schools with a lot of subsidy from the government, and they don't serve the South African patients but rather leave for New Zealand and Australia, if not America and Europe. There are no mechanisms in place under which the desperately needed skills can be channelled, and besides that, our government is subsidising brain drain. There are no rules and laws that enforce doctors to serve the nation; doctors complain too that the South African doctors are poorly paid. Black engineers are also very scarce. South Africans are poorly trained in apprenticeship, hence the high rate of unemployment. Africans from other parts of the continent are taking over jobs that are supposed to be filled by South Africans, a recipe for xenophobia amongst Africans, people from the same stock. All these things are happening right under the nose of the ANC-led government.

8

Africa Needs New Rulers

Europe decolonised Africa in the 1960s. They 'educated' African leaders who were to remain behind and carry forward the program of their former masters, i.e. govern on their behalf. What most African countries called independence or freedom was in fact a change of seats from the European masters to the black elite, and the status quo would remain intact if not changed for the worst. The raiding of the continent continues unabated by this elite, who (most of them) had been educated in American and Western universities. These leaders continue to rule the continent up to this day. They connive under Western political hegemony and their imperialist capitalism while presenting themselves as vanguards of their nation's independence. We all know how the civil liberties of African people are violated in the entire African continent.

When most of the African countries received their independence from their colonial masters, they hoisted new flags. Leaders delivered moving speeches in the name of the people. Promises were made and new hopes were raised and the people on the ground remained optimistic. The masses developed trust in these 'liberators', and they participated in every effort that sought to improve their lives. They are disappointed when the rules of the game began to change; the elites began to flash their newly acquired wealth, some of which obtained through corrupt means. Just like their colonial masters, they drive flashy cars; show off their newly acquired opulence through social gala dinners, expensive designer suits; and buy houses on the land that had previously been earmarked for their masters. While there is nothing wrong in living in the suburbs, some of them exaggerate this affluence by building glass houses and high-fenced walls, while some well-trusted intellectuals drift into their cocoons and sink into permanent silence, pretending everything is well.

Hypocrisy and double standards are very hard to hide as they growl like pit bull terriers when you introduce the subject of a surfacing new oppression in a new dispensation. They control the resources and wield an upper hand in the procurement systems that are giving them access to tenders and kickbacks. They manipulate the tender processes and repel everything that does not tow their political party lines. They control the municipalities where they sink their hands into the cookie jar and embezzle money for their self-aggrandisement right under the nose of their ignorant rank and file. They send their children to private schools, where they pay a fortune, some of which have been acquired through kleptocracy and embezzlement. They see nothing wrong when the education system is brought to a standstill in the country. When African teachers (who usually picket on trivial grievances) go on strike, the leaders of the dominant party will not condemn that action. After all, their children are in the unaffected private and public schools, former model C schools that were built by their former masters.

Many times the unions themselves are part of the alliance with the ruling party. They laugh all the way to the banks, giggling at the jokes that amuse only them. They spend this money in a number of gala dinners, where they cut the deals, and they spend fortunes on breakfasts in the five-star hotels. They do this networking while a fleet of luxurious cars are parked outside these flashy hotels. They dress in designer clothing, and their wrists are glittering with Rolex and Breitling watches, a display of opulence. When their insatiable appetites have been pampered, they buy buffaloes at exorbitant amounts of millions, while children in their villages are learning under the trees and sharing limited books.

They manipulate the laws to suppress the protests of their fellow countrymen, and they give a 'shoot to kill' order to those who are perceived as disturbing the investments of Western multinationals. After all, that is how they show their former masters that indeed their Western capital will be defended at all costs even if it means committing dastardly acts of spilling the blood of their own brethren. At this moment, the opposition, which is occasionally vociferous in pointing out the ills of society and which is predominantly European in appearance, will be visibly silent in condemning the barbaric actions of the ruling party. Their voices will be stronger when, in the same vein of the striking season, the farmworkers employed by white farmers begin to demand better wages; these are the double standards we find in South African politics.

African leaders sit in air-conditioned boardrooms and crack jokes that are lacking in substance and are meant to appease their masters. This is happening while the African miners are sweating like pigs underneath the surface, drilling and extracting gold and platinum, while their leaders are drinking 100 per cent fruit juices and counting the dividends and shares of the unions that are working in cahoots with their former oppressors. The holders of the means of production are using them as their mouthpiece when they want to quell the anger of the proletariat. When the defenceless workers ask for their share in the surplus value of what they were mining, they are brutally put down like wild dogs. These uncouth and barbaric leaders, just like their ruthless former oppressors, have no mercy for the poor who continue to vote for them. They enjoy a renewed mandate to go back to the drawing board to plot the schemes of implanting their devilish ideas again and again.

The same old crooks will keep on returning to the reins of power with a renewed mandate that is obtained from the ignorant masses. The nation was deprived of good education and victims of gutter education that was designed by the colonial masters with the intention of producing a race of underdogs and workers of servitude. Inferior education is entrenched in the ideas of the new African leadership working in cahoots with their Western masters. This is done in order to serve and perpetuate modern slavery. Western capital creates a few African mining magnates and pays a pittance to the exploited workers. The leadership lose their conscience as their hearts and mouths salivate for more and more profits. It is no shame that the protesting miners are gunned down by the police who have been notorious for their brutal killings since their formation as an establishment.

The soil of Africa is drenched with the blood of innocent victims mowed down by the trigger-happy police, who would kill at the orders of profit-makers in cold boardrooms of hot-blooded fat capitalists. When democracy is newly defined, you will discover that genocide and dastardly acts of murder will be committed by the white wolves dressed in black wool. Window dressing is a façade meant to portray African leaders as the holders of the means of production when they are just being used as a conduit to electrify new shock and oppression of their own people.

The recent kidnap of young girls in Nigeria by the Boko Haram is another conclusive proof of bad governance by the African elite. The tardiness of the Nigerian police force shocked the world. The girls were abducted and their dormitories burnt down, but there was no police to respond and give a speedy rescue to them. The government of Goodluck Jonathan was exposed for its failure to respond to the challenges posed by the Islamist militants of the Boko Haram. This group of militants has been harassing the Nigerian citizens for a number of years, and yet there seems to be no solution to combat their aggression. The Boko Haram is in a campaigning spree to rid Nigeria of Christianity and Western education. They hate the reading of books, and they have killed a number of teachers and destroyed villages and small towns. They have done this as if Nigeria was just a jungle with no state.

Once more, an African country has been exposed, with the toothless African Unity unable to assist. The girls were left to the hands of their captors. They were taken against their will and were forced to wear Muslim clothing and recite the Koran. The commander of the rebel forces is threatening to sell them, and the whole world is shocked at this latest violation of the human rights. Once more, their plight was highlighted by the Western media after an outcry of their parents; their government was as helpless as the parents. The Nigerian elite has kept quiet. They haven't called for assistance, and no awareness campaigns were ever launched to galvanise support from the international community. The USA has offered to give strategic assistance. At the beginning of May 2014, they started their reconnoitring expedition, and their fighter jets were already hovering over the stronghold of Boko Haram on 27 May 2014. But the Nigerian general appeared on the television, saying they knew where the girls were kept and that they were not ready to launch an attack because that could jeopardise the rescue mission. He said these words with a facial expression which did not symbolise any sympathy—in short, he was smiling. How inconsiderate!

South Africa kept quiet until the campaigns in Europe and America were gaining momentum. The South African government never condemned this incident until the Bring Back Our Girls Campaign was rife in Europe and the US. The ANC Women's League joined in the bandwagon three weeks after the abduction. The way in which the BBC and the CNN highlighted this barbaric incident put the SABC to total shame. The cruel hoax of the African elite is put to a test one more time. It has been exposed that they do not care about the people they lead until the outside world exposes the truth.

One man's terrorist is another man's liberator. The way in which the African leaders govern the continent leaves much to be desired. The weakness that has been mentioned above is the cause of all human suffering in Africa. Most of the leaders do not take office in order to make a difference for the people on the ground; they take these positions in order to enrich themselves, and if the other group notices that they are getting richer while the nation suffers, they begin to form militant organisations which will then fight to the bitter end. If the aggressive group succeeds in overthrowing the government, the vicious cycle starts again. Corruption becomes rife and embezzlement and self-aggrandisement take the centre stage until another group is formed. Constitutions are there in name only; even the citizens have no understanding of how to use them for their own protection. The elite group uses these documents to protect themselves and their privileges.

The ignorant citizens are used as voting fodders and dumped after the elections. They do not know their strength and the power that they hold until such time that the damage has gone to an extent that the country is already in ruins.

The people receive the government that they voted for. When they are brutalised by insurgencies, such as what is happening in Nigeria and Kenya, they are just caught off guard and defenceless, and that is when the reality surfaces that they have no government. They look at the government officials who are as defenceless as they are and who will only think of their families and their privileges. Africa needs to wake up and learn politics, like the other races of the world who do not take any nonsense from their incompetent leadership.

Recently, we learnt that the people of Senegal were washed ashore by the sea after their attempt to cross the Atlantic to Europe, looking for job opportunities. Africa is the richest continent in the world; one wonders why its children would die of hunger and disease. All that Africa needs is a dedicated leadership, not the leeches who take power for their self-interest. The population of Africa has to look at history in retrospect. Africa needs new rulers.

9

All Power to the People

They say the masses have claimed back power from the educated elite. The ANC had a national conference in Polokwane, where an educated pan-Africanist intellectual, President Thabo Mbeki was removed from power. Mr Mbeki was further recalled from being the president of South Africa, and most of his cabinet ministers resigned. Those who recalled him are saying that the ordinary people were claiming back power from the educated and sophisticated elite. The educated were replaced by a self-taught, less-sophisticated polygamist from Nkandla, KwaZulu-Natal, Mr Jacob Zuma. The 100 per cent Zulu boy is a seasoned politician who is a favourite of many in the ANC rank and file; he didn't spend much time on formal education, and he is a very interesting character to watch. Zuma is very popular with both illiterates and the literates alike. The ANC is claiming to be the most democratic movement in the whole African continent; it boasts of being the oldest liberation movement in the African continent. It was also voted into office by the poorest of the poor, the workers, and the rural peasants. The black middle class, even though it constitutes a smaller number, also voted for the ANC.

The smaller number of the middle class is blamed on the years of deprivation under apartheid, where inferior Bantu education contributed massively to the lack of educated African scholars, intellectuals, professionals, the think tank, etc. Many black people lack the appropriate skills to govern the country on all fronts. The resolutions taken from the Polokwane conference were supposed to address this scourge aggressively. South Africa has a sophisticated capitalist economy with a large gap between the haves and the have nots. There are many people who live below the breadline, and most of them are black. It is this class that continues to pose a serious challenge to the ANC government. The ANC faces a backlog of delivery to the poor, and this is challenged by a number of demonstrations that are always requesting the government to show full commitment in redressing the imbalances from the past.

Educated people are not scarce in South Africa. The only problem is cronyism, which continues to place unskilled people in positions of responsibility. There was a recent South–South cooperation among the BRICS countries, and all members were represented by the leaders with know-how of economics and politics. We kept on wondering what the South African delegation was composed of and what were they saying to their counterparts. When people discuss the issues that touch the future of their countries, they send professors and doctors who have majored in that field, and we just happened to be the only country that sent common people who are not schooled in those particular fields. This happened because power is in the hands of the people themselves; our president is a common person, and most of his ministers in the cabinet are self-taught individuals.

Three tiers of our government are filled with officials whose credentials are seriously doubtful. There are many economic policies that have been introduced in our country, but they have failed to work, so they are never implemented. The opposition is having a feast in all these spheres of government, and I don't see the ANC rectifying this mistake, not in the near future.

Most councillors in the municipalities have failed to acquire at least a matric certificate. One wonders how they debate the complex by-laws of their municipalities, and most of these councillors were selected from the offices of the ANC and introduced to the people as their representatives. Most of them are gatekeepers; they will prevent the slightest initiative of an educated person who tries to introduce progressive programs into their wards, and they will begin to see a dragon trying to snatch a feeding bottle from their families.

Since they are not educated, they have to bow to the dictates of the vagaries of life, and the more their wives and children depend on it, the more tenaciously they will fight for their mandate. This alone will make every other man with political instincts their personal enemies; in every new movement, they will scent the possible beginning of their end and, in every man of any greatness, the danger which menaces them through that man.

One wonders how the ANC plans to achieve the perceived goals of implementation of their policies with this material of leadership. The branches of the ANC are commonly attended by a group of illiterates. As it has been pointed out that the councillors of the ANC are not educated, it should not surprise the reader that almost all of them are the chairmen in their branches (wards). This is done with the intention of avoiding two centres of power, as is noticeable in the president of the ANC, who is also the president of the country. The same holds true with the premiers in their provinces; they are all (perhaps with the exception of Gauteng Province) ANC provincial chairmen. It is up to the reader's imagination to think about the type of politics that goes on in those wards.

While Bantu education was a taboo because of its inferiority, one should salute those Africans who, in the face of brutal repression and deprivation, chose to exercise their patience and went to school and became teachers, lawyers, doctors, and professionals in different fields. There is a common belief that this middle class should be taking the lead in their respective communities, but on the contrary, they are visibly absent. Whether the ANC is repelling them on purpose or it is bowing to the advice of the National Party that keeps black men illiterate and ignorant, they won't ask many questions. It all boggles the mind. Most of the educated people are still puzzled by what was discussed in the Groote Schuur Minute before the talks about talks led to the formation of the constituent assembly called CODESA, where the future of South Africa was discussed.

There is a suspicion that amongst other opinions, the National Party advised the ANC around these four important points:

- Keep the standard of education as low as possible. Black people of African descent should be kept ignorant, and make sure that they remain inferior to other races in their country (do as we have been doing through Bantu education). They must not understand the sophistication of the capitalist system. All that they have to provide is cheap labour—an unskilled and uneducated class that will serve and service the cog of a well-oiled capitalist machine. It is a bad idea to educate an African child; educated people have a tendency to ask too many questions, so in order for you to have a stable and peaceful government, just keep them ignorant. And indeed, black people are the victims of this conspiracy.
- Land is a no-go area in these negotiations. Live it sacrosanctly. Black people should be squashed in townships, while acres and hectares of their ancestral lands remain in the hands of the Europeans—both present and absent landlords. The Europeans controlled Africans using segregationist laws, such as Group Areas Act in 1913 and the influx control laws on black people, which was entrenched as the law that will control their movement from the rural to the urban areas; 87 per cent of the land remained in the hands of the minority of Europeans until 1994. It is not surprising that the ANC government has utilised only 3 per cent of the land which was owned by the apartheid state. South Africa is nearly half the size of Europe, if not more; the recent statistics from the 2012 census revealed that out of the population of nearly fifty-two million people, black people of Africa constituted thirty-seven million, while white people were at four million. The whites owned 82 per cent of the land, while black people in general (i.e. Indians and

coloureds included) shared the other 18 per cent. This is happening after nineteen years of ANC rule. You can drive from Durban to Johannesburg and criss-cross the country from Polokwane to Cape Town, but there is no farm of a black man next to the freeway. The only squatters in this country are the black people; they are called illegal occupants in the country of their own origin. This is noticeable every day, but everyone is minding their own business as if everything else is normal. If this doesn't deserve to be called a conspiracy and a betrayal of their struggle for freedom, what is?

- Control the state apparatus and safeguard the Western imperialist capital. Have an alliance with the strongest federation of trade unions in the country so as to make it easy to contain the militancy of the workers. In return, we will create a safety financial net for you to be able to enjoy the privileges that were previously deprived to you as the African elite. When you use that money, we will cry foul and shout 'Corruption!' when deep in our hearts, we know the name of the game. You will shoot to kill at the miners who disturb our capital. At least, it won't be us who will be doing the shooting. The savages will be taught a hard lesson, and they will learn a thing or two. Show them who is boss.
- Create a welfare state. The masses of women and children will be fed by the state through social grants. You will encourage young girls to get pregnant. The matriculants will swell the ranks of the unemployed by their numbers, and they will be catered for in the youth funds. The unskilled and unemployed will receive their social security, and pensions will be given to the aged. In that way, their dependency syndrome will assist you in securing the cling to power for some time, while the masses vote for you to express their gratitude. The extreme left, such as the PAC and AZAPO, will be sidelined by the process. It will be the ANC and the DA at the centre, and the right and centre of the continuum will operate in a vacuum. The ultras will be in the periphery, crying foul.

This could just be the figment of many people's imagination.

These are the four main pillars within which the anger of the South African masses is contained. Unemployment is very serious in South Africa; there is an overwhelming protest which threatens massive upsurge, and it sometimes makes it imminent for the revolution to start. Recently, we witnessed the police brutally killing protesting miners; the incident at Marikana was the first of its kind under the new dispensation, and it shocked the entire world. The ruling elite gave orders for this recent spate of genocide to be committed.

These are recurring incidents in South Africa which are carried out by the government of the new African leadership. The protest which led to the death of Andries Tatane was meant to address the lack of service delivery, and all police officers who were involved in that killing were recently acquitted on the grounds that there was no sufficient evidence and that the death of this civilian was of his own making. The Cato Manor police squad, which is notorious for their heavy-handedness when dealing with the criminals, are being treated with kid gloves, while the terrorised communities are still trembling at the mention of their name. All these incidents are reminders of the killing squads of the old system and the brutal massacres in Sharpeville and Soweto.

10

Inequality amongst Races

The first bullet point above, which is on education, bears testimony to this. In Durban the largest port in the African continent produces massive amounts of revenue to the GDP of the KZN Province and the GNP of the country as a whole. The Gini coefficient of this city tells a different story; besides that, every sector of the economy is dominated by people of Indian origin. Almost all the heads of departments are Indian. Out of ten million Zulus in the province, there is not even a single one of them who is trusted enough that he can lead a department. In the manufacturing sector of this big city, there is no Zulu man who owns a factory. The Zulus who happened to be the majority in the province of KwaZulu-Natal have no shops in the major cities and towns of their province, and here we talk about the retailers and corner shops as you would find the Koreans in US cities. Indians are holding superior positions in the local government of Durban. They are councillors and speakers; others serve in the EXCO (the highest decision-making body of the city and the outskirts). If this is not a deliberate encouragement of racial tension and a recipe for the clash between races as what has occurred in 1949 between the blacks and the Indians, what is?

When a well-known Zulu theatre artist, the famous *Sarafina!* stage playwright Mr Mbongeni Ngema, wrote a song about this, he was criticised and persuaded by the leaders of the ANC to drop it. It didn't end there; it was banned in the local radio stations. The ANC did it because it ruined their base to campaign for a vote in the Indian areas, and it is a continued lack of trust and confidence in the ability of Africans to lead in the highest positions in their cities. It is believed that Durban is the second place in the world for the Indian people after India. The recent statistics shows that there are many Asian people from Pakistan and Bangladesh who continue to flood Durban. They are opening up their businesses in areas where the Zulus are not allowed.

The KwaZulu-Natal government of the ANC is failing to create a conducive climate under which businesses can thrive for all races. Equality is unknown in this province. Instead, we see Africans from the diaspora opening up some small businesses in Point Road and small salons in the smaller streets of the city, but if a local Zulu man were to try that in his own province, it will be like trying to climb Kilimanjaro in winter while wearing a vest and sandals. All sorts of laws and by-laws will be explained to him until he fully understands that there is no space for a man of his skin colour, a texture of hair, and maybe big flat nose in addition.

There is no place in the world where African people are found to be leaders, especially in countries that are predominantly other races. If, for example, the African people happened to be in India by accident, they will be found digging trenches and working as domestic servants; no black man will ever be found in a leadership position or any other position of influence, for that matter—not in the national parliament, not in the cabinet, not in the senior positions of key institutions in the country, not to mention financial positions. As black people, we are not trusted by other races; no one trusts that we can be competent enough to hold critical positions. This is our position and our experience in this new South Africa under the leadership of the ANC in a new dispensation.

The worst part is that, with the excuse of running short of good leadership, African leaders are always playing second fiddle to other races. It is not only in the field of politics and religion but also in sciences, economics, engineering, etc. In politics, African leadership serves the interests of other races first before that of their own brethren; the ruling party is putting all black buffoons and clowns in positions of responsibility on purpose.

The government of the ANC is a disciple to this theory. In their branches in townships, teachers, nurses, business people, priests and pastors, social workers, doctors, and lawyers are nowhere to be seen in positions of leadership, the BECs (branch executive committees). We are led by a bunch of buffoons who follow every order without questioning. It is no surprise that the Democratic Alliance (the official South African opposition) will always win in the council chambers. The primary school–educated councillors of the ANC cannot match the well-educated researchers of the DA. This mind-boggling modesty of the ANC leaves a number of educated blacks asking themselves with the questions, What is the aim of the ANC in doing this? I insist in reiterating that this frustrating scenario, which has gone on for more than nineteen years, is a result of the secret discussions between the National Party and the ANC as well as the sunset clauses, which had been recommended by the leader of the SA Communist Party, Mr Joe Slovo.

The sunset clauses were introduced to soften the ultra right in the Conservative Party and the AWB, the verkrampte (those who were opposed to change) elements within the National Party as opposed to the verligte (those who were perceived by the verkrampte as leaning towards the left). The white bureaucrats had to be protected in their positions for a transitional period of five years. While Joe Slovo's ideas were good and well thought out, they had to go on for five years while educated black people were doing the understudy. As for the reason why this condition still persists after nineteen years, honestly it boggles the mind. After nineteen years of our so-called democracy, white people are still dictating all terms.

If you are confused by my testimony, here is a shining example. No matter how much President Zuma wishes to keep his cronies in power, if the DA does not approve of it, he will quickly do as they instruct him to do—i.e. kick them out.

Example one: The DA discovered that Mr Jackie Selebi, a stalwart of the ANC and the commissioner of the South African Police Service and a leader of the highly respected international organ of policing (the Interpol), was conniving with the drug dealers and petty muggers. They ordered President Zuma to fire him, he did.

Example number two: The DA privately investigated the movements of Minister Sicelo Shiceka, and they discovered that he had been visiting his girlfriend, who was imprisoned in Switzerland. Shiceka was using the taxpayers' money, which he failed to account for when he was cornered by the DA in parliament. The DA instructed President Zuma to kick him out of office because he was an embarrassment to the South African parliament. This buffoon from Mpondoland was no match for the ecstatic Cape Town corridors of power. Zuma obliged; he did as the DA had given him that instruction. A poor, sickly Mpondo went back to Ngquza, where he died after a long illness.

Example number three: Bheki Cele was suspected by the shadow cabinet minister for safety and security Ms Dianne Coller-Barnard of the DA that he had been trying to manipulate the figures of the state funds meant to buy the building that was supposed to be used by the police as their headquarters. The DA ordered the Public Protector Thuli Madonsela to investigate the matter and instructed President Zuma to get ready to give General Bheki Cele a boot. Zuma presented the arms and cocked the rifle. Msholozi was ready to fire; he told the entire country that after the investigation by the Public Protector, the general had to give him a sound reason why he should not be expelled. If I was in the shoes of Bheki Cele, I would have resigned immediately to save myself from the humiliating embarrassment that was to follow. Instead, the general prepared himself to fight back. When Jacob Zuma asked Judge Baloyi to lead a commission on this matter, General Bheki Cele prepared himself too. The presentation of the matter to the judge was done, and the cross-examination went on. But as the proceedings went by, Judge Baloyi stated in very clear and categorical terms that as a black man, he was so embarrassed. He ran short of saying how disappointed he was; he just wondered how on earth President Zuma offered such a critical position to a man of such low calibre.

The commission went on, with the excitement of the media giving all the coverage, including the fact that General Cele had signed important documents without reading—and the worst part, on a boot of a car! All educated and intelligent black men of South Africa felt like hiding themselves under the tables. The revelation of that complete recklessness and negligence of the worst kind left all of us embarrassed and dumbfounded. Yet the general was expressing himself with super confidence, floundering and waffling like a guilty child. He was found guilty, and the DA was vindicated. Helen Zille told President Gedleyihlekisa Zuma to do the usual—i.e. General Bheki Cele be given the boot. It happened; he was shown the door.

The DA said to President Zuma, 'Good boy.' While the Bheki Cele ordeal was still fresh and lingering in our minds, the DA presented another fish to fry. The Zulu man from Nkandla was still taken aback, trying to figure out what Auntie Helen was about to say. Ms Lindiwe Mazibuko, the leader of the official opposition in the South African parliament, got into the bandwagon. Ms Lindiwe Mazibuko is a darling to all model C students of politics. She is spicing up South African politics. She is fearless and always prepared to take the ANC head on. However, her looks are very similar to those of the wives of President Zuma—and this is my own observation. She is beautiful like the second wife of the president. I am sure that if you were to meet maNtuli in the party and minutes later you meet Lindiwe, you will definitely think they were sisters. With her plump body, she looks like the president's third wife, kaMadiba, while her expressions and gestures are very similar to that of the president's fourth wife, maNgema.

I am sure it sometimes crosses the mind of President Zuma that Lindiwe should be making fire in the Nkandla compound as his fifth wife instead of making noise in parliament, which would disturb a real Zulu man while he tries to govern the country. This mouth-watering, delicious girl (if I may use the words of the man himself) should be taught some manners and respect as defined by African men in general and the Zulu polygamists in particular. Julius Malema saw her as a tea girl for Helen Zille, the madam (as Julius would call Auntie Helen), and ordered Lindiwe around—as is reiterated by the leader of the Communist Party Dr Blade Nzimande in his song titled 'My Mother Was a Kitchen Girl'. I think Juju was a bit harsh. I don't think that Lindiwe had to be relegated to that lower status. That was very demeaning. She is a leader of the opposition party, and she got there on merit.

Enough about the polygamy sense of humour. Jacob Zuma is the pride of many African men as far as polygamy goes; that is my general understanding when I'm socialising with my fellow brothers from the diaspora. Polygamy is not a Zulu thing; all black people are the descendants of polygamy. My own great-great-grandfather, Lehana, the son of King Sekonyela of the Batlokwa tribe had fifteen wives, and King Sekonyela himself had twenty-six wives and a number of concubines. Now, who knows? Maybe one day we will discover that President Zuma is related to the Batlokwa tribe.

Example number four: The DA leader Ms Lindiwe Mazibuko had pointed out that Ms Gwen Mahlangu-Nkabinde had to go—she had been implicated in the Bheki Cele saga—and that she was incompetent. Ms Mahlangu-Nkabinde was the minister of public works; she looked lost each time she was interviewed on matters pertaining to her department. She had complicity to the cooking of figures in the purchase of the block of flats for the headquarters of the police. The whole procurement system was questioned by Public Protector Thuli Madonsela. It appeared in the final analysis that some people were going to reap some rewards in terms of kickbacks. President Zuma was asked by Lindiwe Mazibuko to show his integrity, and indeed Zuma complied. Ms Gwen Mahlangu-Nkabinde was told to switch off the lights and close the door on her way out. These are some of the few examples on how President Zuma plays Uncle Sam to the voice of the predominantly white opposition.

President Zuma recently reshuffled his cabinet after ANC's conference in Mangaung and after all those who supported his political rival, Deputy President Kgalema Motlanthe, were relegated to lower positions—like how the premier of the Limpopo Province, Mr Cassel Mathale, was sent to the national parliament in Cape Town to become an ordinary member of parliament (MP), a backbencher. Zuma was even more ruthless to the minister of human settlement Mr Tokyo Sexwale, who was kicked out of the national legislature and lost his job.

Example number five: This is another puzzling case. There was an outcry in the country that, Mrs Angie Motshekga, the leader of the ANC Women's League and also the minister of basic education, should have been given the boot a long time ago. A few weeks before Zuma's reshuffle, the South African Democratic Teachers Union (SADTU) had organised a few marches around the country, asking President Zuma to show Angie the door. SADTU's protests had been based on the Limpopo book crisis and many other promises Angie had failed to meet. Helen Zille came with her guns blazing in defence of Angie Motshekga. She told Zuma not to listen to the teachers' union, and she gave her own reasons opposing those given by SADTU and in alliance with the ANC.

Zuma ignored the voice of his alliance partners and listened to the leader of the opposition, Mrs Helen Zille of the DA. He didn't fire Minister Motshekga, and as we speak, Mrs Angie Motshekga is still the minister of basic education in South Africa. These are not double standards, as many people would argue; this is called South African politics. President Zuma himself is a son of a domestic servant who served in the kitchens of white madams in the olden days. Zuma knows the meaning of the word *madam*, as he once was a garden boy. It is very good that he respects the white madam rather than listening to the crazy black teachers whose children are taught by the teachers who vote for the DA. President Zuma is intelligent enough to see cheap politics from a distance; he ignored SADTU.

11

Blame It on the Whites

There are always two sides to a story—one that is told as it is and sounds like a gospel truth and one that opposes it and comes out with a different version. The story of the arrival of white people in this continent and things that they did to the indigenous people; the belligerent forces that invaded Africa; the wars waged against the indigenous people of the soil and the taking away of their land; the colonisation, Balkanisation, and oppression that followed afterwards; the brutality that accompanied the seizure of land; the raiding of the countries; the squander of wealth; the raiding of West Africa; and the slave trade.

The other side of the coin is the story that is told by the whites themselves, and it goes thus: Black people were discovered walking naked and had to be clothed and civilised. The indigenous people were ill-treating one another and behaving like savages. They had uncouth and barbaric tendencies starting fighting when meeting one another along the pathways. Women were raped and were not protected by the law since there were no Western laws and institutions such as courts and prisons and no mechanisms to enforce it. Formal education was absent, and illiteracy prevailed. They lacked respect and manners due to their uncivilised ways of doing things. Big families attacked smaller and vulnerable ones who were outnumbered because of the shortage of men and warriors to protect them. And the Europeans cannot be blamed for slavery because the West Africans betrayed one another. There were groups that surrounded able-bodied men and women and sold them to the slave traders. And there were many other social ills going on at the time.

The natives had to be civilised through Christianity and be taught in schools so that they would learn to read and write. They had to be taught Western ways of advanced medicine so that they'd drop their backward ways of medication, such as administering enema, making incisions on their bodies, covering themselves in hot and steamy water, vomiting, etc. All these barbaric tendencies had to be brought to a halt.

African men were doing nothing except training as warriors and going around fighting one another. When there were no tribal wars, they would sit at home and observe women doing their domestic chores. They would drink beer, get drunk, start petty squabbles, and fight one another until someone is maimed or killed. Women were doing everything—going to the fields with babies on their backs, chopping sticks and grass to build their houses, tilling the soil, organising food, cooking, and cleaning their houses—while men were relaxing under the trees, laughing and enjoying food and drinks. These were the stories told by anthropologists and missionaries—the barbaric oppression of women and the enslavement of the natives by others.

When gold was discovered in South Africa, it began a new process of industrialisation. Manpower was needed, and the infrastructure demanded a lot of labour to such an extent that young men had to be recruited from the neighbouring countries. The white men began to make the laws that were forceful, and taxes for the cattle were introduced. Black people were forced to reduce their livestock so that their dependency on cattle would be minimised, forcing young men to go and look for work and earn money. Towns and cities were built, and the lifestyle of black people underwent a complete metamorphosis.

The social structure of the black families was changed from the extended to the nuclear. The reign of the indigenous kings and queens of ancient Africa were brought to an end, and the roles played by the African councillors were completely altered. In the olden days, African politics operated differently. The social patterns and the culture operated differently from what the Europeans knew. The senior members of families used to go to the king's palace, where they will sit in councils and discuss issues in their communities. They would deliberate on social and political matters until they were in agreement with the steps that had to be followed. They will then go to their communities, where they reported back on the decisions taken by the veterans and the old guard of their communities as a collective. This was democracy in the African context.

Social anthropology books through the accounts of writers such as Evans-Pritchard, Lucy Mair, and Malinowski have attested to this version. The Western ways and modernisation affected the African way of doing things. The mushrooming of the townships and rapid urbanisation affected the social stratification of the black communities. Traditional leadership was undermined, and the roles of the traditional leaders were limited by white men's law. In townships, black people began to know that one can argue and oppose the councillors and that leaders are not born but are produced by circumstances, that they can be elected and be mandated, and that they can be removed through the ballot or be forced to step down. They began to know that kings and queens do not hold absolute powers and that they can be dethroned if the need arises.

The whites make their argument in this way, but the Africans continue to debate as they juxtapose both dichotomies.

In South Africa the confusion born out of this rapid change was exploited by the homeland leaders, who used it to entrench their apparatus of authority to the masses of rural people. Legitimate leaders were sidelined or even kicked out of the country. The shining example of this theory was the overthrow of Xhosa Chief Sabata Dalindyebo, who was ousted by the Matanzima brothers, who were governing Transkei. Chief Sabata Dalindyebo had to go to exile and join the ANC. Chief Mangosuthu Buthelezi organised the Zulu tribe, capitalising on the ignorance of the rural masses. Inkatha members were told that the ANC wanted to undermine the traditional structures and that the voice of traditional leaders will be rendered ineffective in the future democratic government, which will be led by the communists and the ANC terrorists. That was why Inkatha warriors acting like vigilantes fought so hard against the liberation of their own people and themselves included.

Vigilantism was organised by the securitate of the South African government, and it was sponsored by the government and the private sector that was opposed to change. Intimidation tactics still persist up to this minute, and many people—even in the townships—still find it hard to understand a person who opposes authority. People know *izinduna* (traditional councillors) in their rural areas, whose words are final. They perceive it as being rude and unruly if an individual voices his opinion that goes against the word of the collective. The Western ways of doing things in politics is still causing a lot of difficulty. From the African perspective, anyone who undermines authority is regarded as a troublesome individual who deserves to be banned, permanently removed from society, or be labelled as a maverick or a rotten potato. The Western politics is ruthless; it teaches people to be individualistic.

The *lekgotla* (Sesotho), *tinkundla* (Swazi), *inkundla* (isiZulu) were the gatherings of the highly respected men in the African society, where serious decisions were collectively taken and disseminated to the nation as a whole. The Western life teaches people to be greedy and cold; nuclear families have destroyed the extended families of the African people, and ubuntu as a concept has no room in our modern society. It's the survival of the fittest and the elimination of the weakest. A child can no longer be the property of everyone in the village. Your child is no longer my child, and this is why today we read of so many bad things happening to young children. African people are no longer caring as they used to be in the olden days. Capitalism has taught them the culture of every man for himself and God for us all.

Capitalism has taught black people that your food, your money, your car, and everything else that you own are yours. If you choose to share it with other people, you will be doing that at your own peril, and you must not cry foul when they vanish after your resources have dried up. It tells us that once a person exceeds the age of twenty-one, s/he or she is no longer a child of the family. If he chooses to visit his parents, he must make a contribution. If he decides to stay in their house, he must pay the rent as a form of contribution. Black people find it hard to believe these things. How can you become a stranger in your own home? These are questions that continue to puzzle them.

Black people find it hard to believe that one man can own hectares and acres of land, while others are squeezed in a tiny piece of space and that one man can own mines of gold and diamond in the country. According to the African way of thinking, things belong to the people, the nation; no man has a right to eat a lion's share, while others receive crumbs and others have nothing to eat. Food must be shared. Land and the deposits underneath the soil belong to the nation and not to private individuals. Water cannot be sold. It is a God-given right, and therefore, it cannot be turned into a commodity. Ubuntu dictates that the resources of the country should be shared equally and that foreigners can be assisted only if they subscribe to the culture and the dictates of that particular African society whether in Ghana, Botswana, or Kenya.

It surprises most people that anyone from outside the continent can just come in as they please and eat the fats of the country, while the indigenous people become mere spectators in their own land. The Chinese own their country, and they run their own economy in China. They own land, where they produce crops for their children and sell the surplus to the outside world. The Indians own India, and all programmes of development and progress are dictated by the Indians themselves.

Europe belongs to the Europeans, and they don't share it with anyone else. They own America, where all other races dance to their tune. They had used force to take away the Americas from the natives. They own Australia and New Zealand, where they decimated the aborigines. They colonised Africa, which is still under their indirect rule, and they own the copper belt of Zambia and the gold of Ghana. They are absentee landlords in the cocoa farms, and they own the oil of Nigeria and all of South Africa's fertile lands and mineral resources. The leadership of Zimbabwe was punished severely by Britain and America when they encouraged their people to grab land from the white farmers. Black people should not own land; those who force this kind of thinking to their people will experience individual sanctions from the West, and they will be punished. Europeans are the conquerors of the world. Anywhere in the world, you will never find them living under Third World conditions. They never stay in an environment where they will be dominated by other races.

The other side of the coin is the account of the Europeans themselves. They are saying you cannot blame everything on the whites. They are not responsible for the suffering of other races in this world. Black people themselves have a lot to learn. White people educated them when they were living in darkness. They were civilised, and yet they still have a number of dictators and despots in their countries. Why don't they learn from the French, that if you are dissatisfied with your dictator, you start a revolution and overthrow him?

African leaders are living in luxurious opulence, and they don't care about their own people. Look at how they have destroyed a country like Congo. Look at the suffering of the people in Mozambique and Angola, where they deposed the Portuguese. Look at how they allow themselves to be used as rebels like Jonas Savimbi's UNITA in Angola and Afonso Dhlakama's Renamo in Mozambique. Look at the suffering of African people in the Great Lakes, the tribal factions and ethnic cleansing in Burundi and Rwanda, and the Tutsis and the Hutus butchering one another for no apparent reason. Look at how they run down their countries, like Uganda, where Idi Amin, the greatest tyrant of all time, plunged the country into perpetual carnage. Annihilation of the infrastructure and genocide in Sierra Leone was not perpetuated by the whites; it was done by African people in a spree of fratricide. It wasn't the whites who were cutting off the limbs of their people. The DRC has been run down, and all the beauty that the Belgians left there has all but vanished.

South Africa is governed by the ANC when the whites are still there. Here is their version: When this country was under their rule, no president of the republic ever built himself a house of 240 million rand with a private clinic and a helipad. No filth and urban decay of this magnitude were ever been noticeable in our cities. These cities had growth. The cranes were everywhere. Buildings were mushrooming all over, and the systems to monitor corruption and kleptocracy were in place. All what we read about these days are corruption; rampant nepotism; crime-infested areas, where thugs rule the day; the strikes and economic disturbances; laziness; and a number of other social ills all over the show. This is just the tip of the iceberg. If we count the number of commissions which have been appointed to investigate African people ill-treating one another, you will notice that it's not the white people who are greedy, have an insatiable appetite, embezzle money, and squander wealth that is meant for the poor.

White people are not the cause of the black people's suffering. They built this country using their brains, energy, and commitment. They are saddened by what they see and cannot take the blame for all the ills that are noticeable these days. They also accentuate that they warned the world about these days. When other African countries were freed, they delayed that process here, and they were right. Had they given Mandela this country in the sixties, they would be trapped in the vicious cycle of poverty, just like the other countries of Africa. The only country that continued to make progress in this continent was South Africa; the whole African continent was plunged into wars, genocide, tribal factions, corruption, embezzlement, squandering of resources, and many other ills that are beginning to take shape in this country. They said that Africans are not fit to govern themselves. Today they have to observe black people run down the country, with load-shedding every day. They fail to understand the basics of economics. They do not do research, and they don't understand that when the demand of electricity forces them to give some to their people in the rural areas, they must also look at the sources of supply so power stations can be built.

When they finally build these power stations, corruption creeps in again. They embezzle money until the amount doubles the initial budget. African leaders manipulate the funds of the government by inviting their brothers, cousins, and sons and telling them to form foundations that are chaired by them and then using government coffers to steal billions in the name of empowering the rural poor when we know that embezzled monies are used for self-enrichment. Do not blame all these things on the whites. When they were governing this country, some of these thieves were in exile, learning and perfecting the art of stealing from their African brothers. A number of African countries are governed by kleptocrats, and that is why their people are flooding to this country. They are coming here because the white people are still here. The whites know black people. They found them in this continent ill-treating one another; they are still doing that. It is not the white people who organised the xenophobic attacks, where the blacks murdered one another like savages. The white people are sick and tired of being blamed for everything that goes wrong in this country.

They are not the ones who are responsible for placing the uneducated into positions of responsibility. If the black people used their franchise qualification to elect a president who has never been to school, why do they blame the whites if things go wrong? Why do they even blame the whites if the same president decides to enrich himself through polygamy and other forms of theft? Where do the whites connect when SABC is led by a person who does not have a matric certificate? Were they ever told to have councillors who haven't completed their primary class sitting on the EXCOs of metros? Are the whites the ones responsible when the black politicians fail to read the financial reports and become a laughing stock to their own people? The whites sit and laugh as they observe these buffoons waffling and floundering, trying to explain themselves, but do notice the sidelining of the educated class that is being replaced by the uneducated and illiterate bureaucrats. How do you expect delivery if bureaucrats cannot read the financial reports and don't know what a balance sheet is?

The whites come from Europe, and their continent is developed because they are serious about life. They are not lazy. They don't depend on handouts. The suffering of the African people is not caused by them. No, it isn't them.

12

Nelson Mandela, the Saint

As I write this book, Nelson Mandela is on the verge of a graveyard. It's been sixteen days since he was admitted to a hospital. Many people are communicating through the social network, speculating that he has already passed on. His family says he is still alive but in a critical condition. I have received a number of calls from friends who think that I might know better. They are asking if the news is true or not. If Madiba passes while I'm still writing this book, may his soul rest in peace. I will always love Nelson Mandela; he is one of my few heroes in this world.

Recently I was rebuking some of my friends who have begun to say Nelson Mandela was a traitor, that he betrayed black people, and that he negotiated the new dispensation for his own fame—and indeed he received the Santa Claus treatment from the West. He made a deal with the whites for them to retain the land, and the sunset clauses were an assurance that white people would continue to hold superior positions in the country. Those who wanted to leave their post would receive golden handshakes, and white criminals would not be prosecuted. This would be done in the spirit of reconciliation and nation-building. They say black people received a raw deal and that Mandela should take all the blame.

I am vehemently opposed to this kind of thinking. I also think that many people are confused by the corrupt leaders of the ANC. Nelson Mandela stood very firm for the ideals of the forefathers of the ANC. He stood high for the principles of a free society and the rights of an individual to participate freely in the economy of the country and politics in a conducive climate. He did what was in his power. He fought for our freedom, while the Bantustan leaders were enjoying the remnants of what had been eaten by their masters. He could have chosen this route; in fact, he was offered that opportunity to run Transkei as the president, but he refused.

As a lawyer, he could have served with loyalty until he was promoted to be a judge, but he refused to be persuaded towards this kind of thinking. He was arrested and sentenced to life imprisonment on Robben Island. While he was there, he tolerated being treated like a slave in the quarry until the ducts in his eyes were affected and his lungs were weakened by pleural effusion, which is the cause of the illness that has kept him in his deathbed as we speak. When he was incarcerated, he remained steadfast in his stringent convictions. He insisted that a man in captivity cannot negotiate his release with his captors. Nelson Mandela was able to conquer the moral high ground, and he defeated his enemy without weapons of mass destruction.

He is a hero to many people in the world in general and the people of the African continent and the diaspora in particular. He delivered a number of statements to the aghast of his enemies. He taught his enemies and the entire world that peace can be achieved without any bloodbath. He has proved to be altruistic on numerous occasions. He sacrificed a portion of his salary for the formation and funding of the Children's Foundation, leaving behind an excellent record of philanthropy. He always insisted that he was a loyal member of the African National Congress, and he worked with other leaders as a collective. He was not larger than life as many dictators in the world would have done in his instance, taking advantage of their fame and popularity.

Anyone who says Mandela was a sell-out has no clue of what he is talking about and should have his head examined. Mandela followed the principles of the ANC with maximum loyalty. After all, the ANC has achieved what it had fought for. Anyone who is dissatisfied with the ANC and the new government of SA must reread all documents of the ANC and discover that there is none whatsoever that says the ANC shall seize power with arms and that they shall take away land from the Europeans. The ANC and Nelson Mandela did their bit, and it is left to other people to go the extra mile and demand the things that the ANC has failed to provide—things such as the disproportionate allocation of wealth, free education, expropriation of land, etc. But a man who spent a quarter of a century in prison, sitting there for his stringent convictions, refusing to be diverted from his set goals, and not budging on the road to freedom, a man who could not be persuaded to go astray—to accuse such a man is wholly incorrect, and it will find no ground in the hearts of many decent people in the world.

No one is able to tell us what he would have done had he been in the position of Nelson Mandela. When Madiba went to prison, he was insisting that he wanted the oppressor to sit down and discuss the future of his country. The enemy was not ready to do that. The whites-only government was not prepared. When Madiba went to prison, there was a vacuum in the politics of resistance, and when young activists such as Steve Biko and Onkgopotse Tiro tried to close the gap, they were brutally murdered. The enemy wanted to negotiate in his own time, dictating the terms and the outcome of the negotiations. The National Party wanted to negotiate from a position of strength.

When Mandela and the ANC agreed to go to the negotiating table, step one of our freedom was achieved. All disenfranchised South Africans won their right to vote. The mandate was given by the people of South Africa, and an overwhelming majority said they wanted to be led by the ANC. Anyone who held a different opinion must convince the masses by organising them until they were given the mandate to lead. But right now, we are stuck with the ANC, and as Nelson Mandela lies on his deathbed, he knows very well that his conscience is clear. He will die a peaceful death, having done all that his gods had created for him to do. May his soul rest in peace.

13

Crime

Crime is very rife in South Africa. People of all races are living in fear. There is violent crime by muggers and killers all over the show. You hear things that are hard to believe. A man was robbed of his cell phone and killed. A woman was gang-raped and brutally murdered; a security guard discovered her mutilated body parts and her disembowelled stomach lying behind the project of a new RDP house in Cape Town. Shocking, isn't it?

A child of eight years, who went missing two weeks before, was discovered next to the river with a slit throat; she had been raped, strangled, and her underwear forced into her vagina. A man was left for dead when a hijack took place; the hijackers took off with his son inside the car. The police issued an amount of 50,000 rand for anyone who can provide information. A car was forcefully taken from a woman, who pleaded for her toddler to be left behind, but the criminals dragged the child and left the car next to the shops; the child died.

There was a series of events in KwaZulu-Natal where young men of teenage years raped women as old as their grandmothers. There were more than four incidents where old women have been raped. The cases were reported between September 2012 to March 2013. Most of these old people lived on their own, and some were as old as ninety years.

Rich people have sheltered themselves in the suburbs, and most of them have surrounded their houses with high walls and electric fences. They carry panic buttons while they are inside their houses. The beauty of their houses is shadowed by the silhouettes of their high walls. Others hire private security to look after their properties. Most of the CCTV cameras in Johannesburg have showed us very disturbing pictures of people being stabbed while they were coming back from work.

Car owners and drivers are victimised in parking areas and at traffic lights in a smash-and-grab frenzy, where the thugs throw themselves at the windows and quickly grab whatever item while the victim is still taken aback. Although car hijacking is no longer as common as it used to be in the nineties, there is a new trend of people who buy your car while you are still driving it. They send thugs to look for a car which is similar to the one they are looking for either because they want some spare parts or they want to change the whole car and use fraudulent means to change registration. This is very common in South African townships.

South Africans are not free. They are very scared of one another. A black man is the most feared animal out of all the species you will find in this country. As a teacher myself, I have noticed that you don't need to be a thug in order to be feared. There have been incidences on numerous occasions where I have observed the behaviour of white women when I am following them in shopping malls. They will walk in front of me, minding their own business until such time that they notice a black man behind them. Their first reaction will be to hold their bags tightly followed by a faster walk and then a change in directions, or they will simply slow down and quickly look at the window and pretend as if they were window shopping in the immediate shops. I used to be offended by these actions before, but I've just come to accept that they are scared of a black man. My friends have related similar stories.

My academic qualifications, certificates, diplomas, and degrees, and the fact that I am a professional person—all these achievements don't matter in the least. I was born black. This is not the case for white women only; my own black sisters do not trust me. At one stage, I made an example in class while I was teaching English, and I asked young black girls this question: 'Let us assume you are walking towards a dark tunnel on a Monday, and you notice a white man entering the same tunnel on the opposite end; on Tuesday, an Indian man; on Wednesday, a coloured man; and on Thursday, an African man. Which day were you too scared to enter the tunnel?' All of them in unison said it was on Thursday. It didn't surprise me. That was exactly the response I was expecting. You can imagine what it is like to not be trusted by all races in the world and, one more nail in a coffin, to not be trusted by your own womenfolk.

This is not surprising because as black teachers, we have heard about a number of cases where educators had sexual intercourse with young girls. We do not hear about these things in the predominantly white schools and former model C schools. Our own wives have no faith in us. Even if this is not a general statement, there are many incidents where we have heard of men impregnating their stepdaughters and even incest with their own daughters, something which was unheard of when we were growing up in this country. Judges, priests, pastors of different faiths, and even principals of schools have been accused of rape. This is a serious test of our moral fibre. The people who are leading the moral regeneration programmes are themselves complicit to this crime.

It is not uncommon in South Africa to hear that a three-year-old girl was raped either by an unknown man or by her own uncle. Rape has lowered the dignity of black men. There are men's forums all over the country, and there are efforts to combat the scourge, but it appears to be escalating to unprecedented levels. Drugs and crime in the Cape Flats have been the stories in tabloids. Instead of our leaders joining hands and fighting the disease in the Western Cape, they are busy debating whether there should be a deployment of troops or a reinforcement to the police force. The residents in this area are locking themselves indoors in fear of the gangs that have taken control of their lives.

Theft and corruption in the government departments are not surprising any more. Our government is failing us. Many people have decided not to report criminal activities in their areas. Others are taking the law into their own hands; they don't trust the police any more. We have a government which cannot protect its own citizens. The Bible says, 'When evil people are in power, crime increases. But the righteous will live to see the downfall of such people' (Proverbs 29:16).

Two of my own cars and an expensive mountain bike that I used for training have been taken away by thieves. I have reported three housebreakings to the police station. I have case numbers from the local police stations, and all these cases have never been investigated. It is just the taking of statements from the victims for statistical purposes. There are no investigations and no arrests even if you tell the police that you know where the culprits live. Crime has ruined the lives of many people. The international investors are now wary to do business in SA.

The sad part is that we have a minister of sport in SA. At first, I felt happy that a calibre of a young ANCYL leader had been appointed to lead this department, but later as time went on, the usual disappointment began to haunt me again. Young men are always blamed for crime. They are accused of standing in township shops and doing nothing. They are blamed for drinking intoxicating liquors and using stupefying drugs. Because of all the illegal substances, such as nyaope or whoonga, cocaine, hashish, dagga, and Ecstacy, our young people have been turned into thieves, muggers, killers, rapists, and thugs. They are accused of idleness and engagement in deviant behaviour. SA is one of the richest countries in the world. Had it not been because of poor leadership, these youths would be competing at an international arena and winning gold medals on all angles.

I have not seen Mr Fikile Mbalula opening sports centres in both urban and rural areas. SA is not only endowed with amazing talent but is also a harp for resources and money. Recently, one of the 800-metre athletes who participated in the Olympics, Mr Ezekiel Sepeng, was quoted protesting about the closing down of the Athletics South Africa (ASA). He pointed out that our South African athletes were going to miss a chance of participating in the championships in Barcelona and that they have to forget about taking part in the Olympics. Although this was a true observation, he missed the chance of saying ASA was closing down because of corruption and embezzlement. ASA was managed by people who were not South Africans at heart and only got their positions because of money and self-enrichment.

Another fascinating fact which needs to be swallowed bitterly as it tastes is that ASA was formed when this country was governed by white people. The outcry was that they were discriminating black people on the basis of skin colour. It should be noted that it was well managed, and it was able to produce African athletes, such as Willie Mtolo, Zithulele Sinqe, Sydney Maree, Thomas Magawana, and many others. It was producing world-class swimmers, and long-distance runners such as Zola Budd were able to take the world by storm. The protest of black people was that they were deprived the chances to partake equally with their white counterparts and that there were no resources in their townships.

The ANC government has been in power for twenty years, and yet you still notice the same disproportionate allocation of resources, and the outcry of deprivation is very much still with us. Mr Trevor Manuel, the former finance minister who is now running the economic desk in the office of the president, was recently heard as saying that we cannot blame apartheid any more as we are now in charge of our destiny. COSATU nearly roasted him alive. Instead of taking their time to try and understand the context under which the statement was made, they simply dismissed what he said as uncalculated hogwash.

The minister of sports forgets that there are means and ends in this world, that you cannot appear to be appreciating the white athletes as they win gold medals at the Olympic Games when you have not done your job of developing the townships and rural areas of the previously disadvantage communities. Again, if we go back to Hezekiel Sepeng's statement about the defunct ASA. Minister Mbalula should be warned that the death of this association is not going to prevent white athletes from competing abroad; it's only black people who are not going there. White people are organised in their smaller organisations and their communities, and the private sector is not wrong in sponsoring their efforts of grooming the talents of their young ones.

White people love their children. They spend time grooming and nurturing a young talent; fathers invest their time watching, encouraging, and supporting their sons in the sports field. I have noticed this eagerness when my son was involved in hockey and football. Even when the model C school is predominantly black, you will notice the happiness in the blue eyes of young Craig or Oscar as he plays in front of his dad. Themba and Dumisani's father will be visibly absent; the minister of sports who happen to be black (if I may remind him) has to encourage his colleagues in parliament that they must go and watch their sons when they play. There is no room for excuses, and the nation, especially of black men, is not going to be built by meetings which are attended in order to avoid family responsibility. He must not appear to be loving and hugging Chad le Clos, who is a product of a loving father; he must remember that somewhere in a KwaMashu street, there is a swimmer who matches Chad le Clos equally.

When we tell the black rouges and rascals to stop smoking dagga and stop going around mugging and killing people, we must also offer them alternatives. The minister must mobilise resources because sports alone can offer thousands of jobs and deviate millions of black boys from activities of crime. Community halls, school halls, and green fields in townships can be harnessed to galvanise young talent into action. He must further talk to his party about councillors who refuse these facilities, gatekeeping because of fear for their positions. If you come up with these solutions, they just perceive you as a threat who wants to usurp power, and as a result, we have a high rate of crimes.

You cannot tell a criminal who became a thug by default to stop sniffing whoonga and then offer him no solution that will rehabilitate him. He will turn back to these substances and hate you. Black boys are not born as thugs, and it does not mean that if you deprive resources to those with lesser melanin, they won't become criminals. Poverty and bad behaviour are enemies of all races alike. It's not a secluded curse to those with stronger pigmentation; otherwise, England will have no white prisoners in their jails.

14

The Problem Child

Julius Sello Malema became the president of the ANC Youth League. Growing up in Limpopo, he was inspired by the firebrand Peter Mokaba. He had been leading the Congress of South African Students (COSAS). When Julius was elected the president of the ANCYL, he revived the spirit of radicalism that had been extinguished by the modest era of Thabo Mbeki. Peter Mokaba had been a fire-eater when the ANC was in exile. He coined the slogan 'Kill the boer, kill the farmer', which didn't augur very well for the right-wing extremists, especially the Conservative Party and the AWB. It failed to impress the ANC moderates at this time. Julius Malema subscribes to this slogan; he has been to court for having rejuvenated it. He has encouraged the youth to revive it because according to him, it is still relevant.

Mokaba's actions caused Thabo Mbeki to summon Peter, and he gave him a short lecture and a tongue-lashing. This led to the silence of Peter Mokaba; he was muzzled in this way, and he chose to serve the government under Mandela and Thabo Mbeki as a 'good, quiet boy'. When Thabo Mbeki came to power, Mokaba was as humble as a sheep. Eugene Terre'Blanche had tried to call Peter to order when Mokaba reminded him that he had the facial features of a black man with his big flat nose and that, racist as he was, he had to look at himself in the mirror and it will surprise him how he resembled a Zulu man from Nkandla. Terre'Blanche got the message correctly.

Julius Malema became instrumental in the efforts to oust President Thabo Mbeki, and he became a staunch supporter of Jacob Zuma. When Zuma was facing a rape trial, Julius was next to him, giving all the support he could. He was heard by the nation saying he would kill for Zuma. It was as if a young man had come back with a vengeance; he wanted to ensure that Mr Thabo Mbeki, who had muzzled his role model and his mentor, is literally kicked out of power and that he faces a cold weather in the political wilderness.

When the ANC went to Polokwane for their conference, the youth under Malema's leadership had been lobbied accordingly. They were able to remove Thabo Mbeki as the president of the ANC, and he was replaced by Jacob Zuma, the former deputy president. Jacob Zuma had been deputising Thabo Mbeki until he was kicked out of office for having been involved in a number of corruption cases—the rape trial and for having received a bribe in the controversial arms deal. Jacob Zuma pleaded not guilty to all charges, including the ones where Schabir Shaik (his financial adviser) had been convicted for. Jacob Zuma became the president of the ANC and later the president of the country.

As time went on, the relations between Jacob Zuma and Julius Malema went bitter and sour. The members of the youth league, including Floyd Shivambu and Ronald Lamola, began to make proposals for the economic freedom of black people in particular. Julius Malema became the advocate of nationalisation of mines and a complete overhaul of the South African capitalist system. Ms Susan Shabangu, the minister of mineral resources, said that it won't happen while she was still alive; she gave an assurance to the foreign investors that nationalisation was not the policy of the ANC and that it never was.

The young lions were a bit disturbed by this response, which they found to be blatantly arrogant and anti-progressive. They went berserk and stated that Ms Shabangus' argument was not holding water since the clause of the Freedom Charter stated that all gold and other mineral deposits under the South African soil belonged to all the people of South Africa. The Freedom Charter had been adopted by the ANC in the Congress of the People in 1955 at Kliptown. And according to the resolutions adopted at the Polokwane conference in 2007 when Zuma became the new ANC president, these clauses were written in black and white, and the whole conference had agreed that they will honour and implement them, so they wondered why there was this latest somersault.

The youth felt betrayed by this double standard. On one hand, the government promised the people of South Africa that they were going to improve their lives by nationalising the mines, and on the other hand, they told the foreign investors to rest assured that their profits would be safeguarded because the issue of nationalisation was not on the government's agenda. The ANC's General Secretary Gwede Mantashe had assured the international investors that this matter was not in the ANC's priority list, that it was not a matter for discussion, and that it was not going to happen any time soon.

The youth was full of rage. They began to criticise the ANC as if they were an opposition party. They proposed that Gwede Mantashe be replaced by Fikile Mbalula in the following Mangaung conference. Mbalula is the former president of the Youth League and the minister of sports under Zuma's cabinet. The Youth League began to go against any word that was uttered by President Zuma, and they continued to undermine everything that came from the Luthuli House (the headquarters of the ANC).

It has been pointed out that anyone who becomes stronger than the ANC should brace her/himself for a bitter outcome. The ANC deals harshly with the people who become larger than the organisation. It happened to Winnie Madikizela-Mandela, it happened to Dr Allan Boesak, it happened to General Bantu Holomisa, and it even happened to the People's Poet, Mzwakhe Mbuli. The mud-slinging process had already started; it began by turning Julius Malema and his comrades into the new victims.

The ANC Youth League was reminded that although it was autonomous to a limited degree, it still had to account to the mother body, which is the ANC. The conversation on the curtailment of the powers of the Youth League was discussed at length by the ANC. The Youth League was fast becoming unruly and plunging the ANC into a new crisis. Julius and his comrades were putting the party into disrepute, and his failure to observe the protocol was further exacerbating factionalism and putting the organisation's welfare at stake. He had to be disciplined.

The ANC sent all the big guns to try and drum up some sense to the young man's mind, but it all fell on deaf ears. Julius continued with his campaign to discredit President Zuma and his entire government. The Julius saga divided the ANC; there were camps within the party, and his maverick style was becoming unbearable to his elders. Instead of toning down his radical speeches, he exacerbated the situation by organising a youth march to the Union Buildings. In this march, Malema wanted to demonstrate to his elders that he commanded massive support amongst the members of the youth. The march was a long walk from Johannesburg to Pretoria; its theme was 'Economic freedom in our lifetime'. It was attended by more than 20,000 young people who proudly walked the entire distance; the outcry was about jobs and economic freedom in our lifetime.

This defiance by Julius was interpreted by the supporters of Zuma as an open confrontation against their leader. The veterans of Umkhonto we Sizwe (the military wing of the ANC), which was led by a certain Mr. Mavundla from KZN, began to issue out death threats to the young man. They said they won't tolerate any unbranded calf who causes factionalism within their glorious movement and that they were fed up with the insults hailed against their commander-in-chief, Jacob Zuma.

These threats fell on deaf ears. Julius decided to unleash more venom as he insulted the president, calling him an illiterate Zulu man. He responded to the death threats by saying it never was in the history of Umkhonto we Sizwe to go around killing people simply because they had dissenting views to those of the mainstream of the ANC. When Umkhonto we Sizwe was formed and first commanded by Nelson Mandela, it had no policy of indiscriminate killing; in fact, its initial activities were based on sabotage of government installations, such as power stations, posts offices, pylons, etc.—not human beings. He said Mr. Mavundla should speak for himself, not for the people's army, and that they should stop promoting ethnic cleansing that anyone who is not a Zulu would then be silenced by threats. He further stated that Umkhonto we Sizwe had been instructed by the commander-in-chief, Comrade Nelson Mandela, to cease their military activities so as to allow the peace process to prevail while the negotiations were taking place, so there was no Umkhonto we Sizwe operations except for a few buffoons who were promoting Zulu dominance over other tribes.

The same sentiment had been expressed by General Sphiwe Nyanda, the former chief commander of Umkhonto we Sizwe, in his opinion in the newspaper *City Press*. He said the activities of the armed forces were suspended due to the entry into negotiations. He further advised those who were still using Umkhonto as their weapon that they were doing this against the peaceful agreements reached at Kempton Park in the CODESA talks.

The ANC began to come up heavily on Julius. A disciplinary committee was formed, led by Mr Derek Hanekom. He was given time to write the terms of reference, and the case commenced. Julius Malema, Sindiso Magaqa, and Floyd Shivambu were found guilty, and they were suspended and given a chance to show remorse. Many people expected Julius to apologise and ask for another chance and perhaps come begging cap in hand for forgiveness. Instead of showing remorse, Julius continued with his fireworks and lodged an application for the matter to be reviewed by the National Executive Committee (NEC). He challenged the verdict by becoming adamant in his convictions, defying every clause of the verdict. The ANC looked at his appeal and requested Mr Cyril Ramaphosa to deal with the matter. Ramaphosa found Malema guilty, and he was expelled from the ANC.

A number of criminal cases against Julius followed, including amongst others money laundering, tax evasion, corruption, etc. The ANC tried to draw a wedge between himself and other members of the executive of the ANCYL. Ronald Lamola, a young attorney who was leading the Youth League at that time, had been very supportive of Julius, and he was one of the eloquent candidates of the concept of economic freedom in our lifetime. But he later showed a moderate stance when he was asked about his support and loyalty to Julius. He told the rank and file not to go to courts in support of Julius and his criminal cases. He said Julius was prosecuted for his personal lifestyle and that his cases had nothing to do with the ANCYL.

In those months, Julius had been slowly jettisoned, and the reports on the media had slowly dwindled. The political wilderness had isolated him to the periphery, and he was later followed by the vagaries of constant prosecution and asset forfeiture. His incomplete mansion was auctioned, and many of his assets were confiscated in order to pay what he owed SARS. The powers that be had gathered that Julius was beginning to work on a farm that he had purchased from a Limpopo farmer. They then sent a man of the hammer to confiscate the farm and put it on auction. Julius had been stripped of all his sources of income.

On 1 July 2013, Mr Ashraf Garda of the SAfm conducted an interview where he featured Julius Malema. He asked him about his thoughts on the fact that the ANC's heavy-handedness was tackling him head on, and Julius mentioned all the things that were taken away from him. He spoke about his latest quandary and the mess he found himself in. He further emphasised that they followed him when he was trying to start a new life in a farm and that they confiscated that farm, and he was being pulled back to active politics again. He stated that he was about to form a new political party, Economic Freedom Fighters.

Ashraf asked him about the manifesto of his party, and Julius stated that the land has to be distributed equally to all citizens of the country. The persistent ill-treatment of the black peasants shall come to an end and that the arrogant whites who continue to persecute African people must brace themselves for something that was coming. Black people in general should participate in the economy of South Africa, and African people in particular should take over and be in total control of the economy of their country. The mines will be nationalised, and the new economic policies will be drafted to favour African people. Education will be equal to all races; it is going to be on the priority list. All those who serve under his government will be remunerated accordingly, but they must remember that they are serving the nation and not their stomachs. He substantiated his theory by saying that he was presently reading about Thomas Sankara.

Sankara was one of the rare African leaders who took over the reins of power at the age of twenty-one. He had restructured his government in Burkina Faso. Thomas Sankara told his ministers and government officials that since they were working for the nation, they were expected to lead by example. The benefits that were enjoyed in the previous corrupt government were taken away. No government official will fly with a business-class ticket unless he upgrades it from economy to business class. He has to do this by digging from his own pocket. When they are abroad, they must sleep in the cheapest bed and breakfast instead of luxurious five-star hotels.

They must drive simple cars, such as Toyotas, rather than expensive Mercedes cars. They must live in simple houses and hostels built by their government. If they want to upgrade that, they must add their own money. There must be transparency and accountability to all, and anyone who goes against that should cease to call herself/himself a leader of the people. Leadership is not meant for self-enrichment, and people should not think that they will be treated with kid gloves if they are discovered to have embezzled money. In countries like China, corrupt people are handed over to the firing squad. There will be no squandering of resources that are supposed to serve poor people, and his government will not tolerate kleptocracy; the times of gravy trains has to come to an abrupt end.

When Sankara's government proved to be a success, it was alleged that the CIA orchestrated his removal from power, which ultimately led to his death. Sankara's government was a model for Africa, and with the fact that he wanted the resources of Burkina Faso to benefit those who were less fortunate, he was then perceived as standing against Western imperialism. He had to be removed permanently from society, and indeed, it happened.

When Ashraf asked Julius if he hated the whites, Malema responded with an astounding no. He said he was brought up under the principles of the ANC, and he further stated that there won't be any reprisals. 'White South Africans are arrogant, it is this arrogance which is safeguarded and pampered by the ANC that annoys me the most.' When asked if the whites can join his party, he responded by saying yes, but only if they abandoned their arrogance and come to the party fully prepared to serve with loyalty. The ANC has preserved the system of apartheid, and black people continue to suffer as if they were still under a racist white government. The ANC continues to protect the interests of the whites at the expense of the suffering black majority. All these have to come to an end. His party will come as a pyrrhic endeavour, owing to all the difficulties people like him went through. Julius is not budging; he is prepared to fight to the bitter end, and he is determined to triumph against all odds.

President Jacob Zuma had once said that Julius was a good, up-and-coming young man who will one day become a leader of South Africa. Julius himself had once burst out with anger and told Debora Patta of eTV that one day he would lead the ANC, assessing the support that he enjoys from young people who think like him and those who felt that freedom in South Africa is still a far-fetched utopia. It looks as if the day of atonement is coming. The clouds are gathering on the ANC, which appears to be slowly attenuating at the emergence of Mamphela Ramphele's Agang, the socialist party which was born out of the brutal killings of the Marikana miners; the Economic Freedom Fighters and the smaller groups of the civil society which objects the governance of the ANC; the renegade group which broke up from the ANC's military wing, Umkhonto we Sizwe, and formed South Africa First. That the ANC will govern until the return of Jesus Christ is left to be seen.

The 2014 election went on fairly well even though some other things, such as the chairlady of the IEC, were casting some doubts to the opposition. When General Bantu Holomisa, the president of the UDM, accused Pansy Tlakula of corruption and requested President Zuma to remove her from the IEC office, the ANC supported her and accused the opposition of stirring unnecessary trouble before the election. Pansy Tlakula had been found by the public protector to be unfit for the position of leading the IEC. She had been found to have been engaged in the activities of corruption which involved her spouse. Pansy Tlakula challenged the verdict of the public protector, and the matter went to court after the election, where she was proved wrong. She has since resigned. Bantu Holomisa's accusations were proved to be correct, and both Holomisa and his allies were vindicated.

Julius Malema's party had been formed and launched in Tembisa in front of thousands of supporters. It has adopted red overalls and berets, domestic servant uniforms for the women activists and members. They were voted by more than a million sympathisers, and they received 6 per cent of the national vote. When Julius Malema was interviewed by Justice Malala of the *Justice Factor* on eTV and by Ashraf in the SAfm, he pointed out that the times of dozing and sleeping in parliament was over for the ANC. It looks as if the prodigal son had returned with a vengeance. In the first few weeks of their entry into parliamentary politics, the EFF had already begun to make their presence felt.

Floyd Shivambu of the EFF called Dr Blade Nzimande, the minister of higher education, by his name. This action didn't augur very well for Ms Thandi Modise, the speaker of the house and chair of the NCOP session. She requested Floyd to retract his statement and prefix the word *honourable*. Floyd vehemently refused to retract from his original position and later showed a book on parliamentary principles that there was no mention of the word *honourable*, that he cannot be ordered to call members of the house *honourable*, and that more than anything, there was no one in the ANC who deserved such a decent word as *honourable*.

The EFF has been kicked out of the House of Assembly by the female speakers of the ANC. The EFF members was accused for their fascist behaviour in parliament in the incident where they asked President Zuma when he was going to pay back the money that the public protector had ordered him to pay. When Zuma was still thinking how he was going to respond to the question of the EFF, Ms Baleka Mbete, the speaker of the house, had come to his rescue by answering that the matter was currently under discussion in the rightful houses of the legislature. The EFF MPs didn't take this lying down. Anarchy ensued as they all shouted, 'Pay back the money!' The speaker ordered them to get out of the house. They refused, and the session in parliament was brought to a standstill. And for the first time in South African history, under the new political dispensation, the house was brought to a halt, held to ransom by the new kid on the block, Julius Malema, and his party, the EFF.

The DA, which is known for being the strong voice of the opposition, was dwarfed by the fierce opposition of the EFF. Julius announced to the South Africans that indeed no one is ever going to doze again in parliament. He is prepared to keep everyone on their toes. This action has also earned him new enemies, such as the commanders of Umkhonto we Sizwe veterans, led by Kebby Maphatsoe, who has openly told Malema that he will be killed.

It didn't end there. While the committee was discussing the terms of reference on how the parliamentary procedures were to be followed, Mr Floyd

Shivambu created a stalemate on who was eligible to chair the meeting. Mr Charles Nqakula, one of the highly respected stalwarts of the ANC, fell into the trap that a young man had created for him. He lost his temper and reminded Floyd that he had joined the ANC and Umkhonto we Sizwe in order to kill anyone who stood in the way of freedom and his people, a gesture that many people who respected Nqakula strongly felt that he was stooping very low, especially because he had said these words inside parliament. You don't correct the mistake of a young man who could be at the age of your son by uttering wrong words. The young man dug a pit, and Nqakula fell into it, thus destroying and tarnishing his reputation and his record of years of good service to the South African public.

Floyd Shivambu was unmoved. Instead, he responded calmly to this old communist and told him that he was not scared by what he had said; he was not going to be frightened by these latest threats. Floyd had previously caused another fracas in parliament when he refused to retract the words that he had used on another ANC member of parliament in calling him a liar. When Baleka Mbete, the speaker, asked him to withdraw the word *liar*, he asked her to give him the word of how to tell someone that he was not speaking the truth.

The EFF has changed the face of parliament in South Africa. Floyd closed the chapter by showing Mr Cyril Ramaphosa, the deputy president of the ANC, the middle finger. This happened after EFF had raised a motion in parliament asking the deputy president to resign; this followed his involvement in the massacre of the people in Marikana. They were again asked by the speaker to vacate the chambers.

On 12/11/14 the South African parliament was brought to a halt when the EFF MP called the president of the country a thief. The situation became tense when the speaker ordered the riot police to come and kick her out. Parliament has been turned into circus ever since the entry of the new kid on the block. Julius Malema and his crew are raining down on the ANC with a vengeance. The MPs of the ANC have wanted to physically beat up the members of the EFF. Lindiwe Zulu (ANC MP) is one of such examples. She was hunting down members of the EFF. They are also enjoying the game when they see the older ANC cadres stooping low to the level of stupid aggression. Maybe, as Julius said, 'there will never be any dozing again in parliament.'

Conclusion

Oppression and liberation are two components of a political life that are very hard to define. There is a thin line between the two of them. People normally say it is easy when you are oppressed because you know who your enemy is. It becomes harder when you are 'free' because you can no longer differentiate between your former oppressor and your 'current liberator'. Sometimes the lines are blurred to such an extent that the system under which the enemy camp operated remains intact to a degree where one cannot tell whether the changes have been effected or if the status quo remains. In the case of South Africa and apartheid, the transfer of power occurred between a white minority government to a black elite group, and oppression persists on the side of the black masses who were previously disadvantaged.

The National Party designed and implemented the evil system of apartheid. We all know that this system was built on the foundations of racial segregation, discrimination, and colour bar. Under apartheid, a white man is above everything that lives in South Africa. Whiteness carries with it a supremacy of the highest degree, which denotes that white people are superior in nature and by their birthright, which is still the case right now. This white supremacy implied black inferiority, and the deprivation of rights to black people took away their dignity and self-esteem. Africa, as we all know, by de facto is a continent of black people; it is the land of their ancestors. In short, African people had existed in this continent since time immemorial. They strode triumphantly in the land of their ancestors like lions in the jungle.

Then came the Europeans, and a serious struggle ensued. Powerful weapons were used in the colonial wars, and African people were defeated. The Europeans conquered Africa, uprooted the children of Africa, and enslaved them in the Americas. Those who remained behind—just like their brethren in the diaspora—experienced brutality of the worst kind under the colonial rule. The scramble for Africa was a process where the Europeans fought on their own over this continent and finally made peace amongst themselves and then started to divide the continent, setting up new colonial borders, giving the African countries their own names, exploiting their riches, and mining the mineral resources deposited underneath the soil of those countries.

They further identified certain black people and gave them scholarships to study in Europe and America. After the colonial wars of resistance, they handed over political power to the black elite. They also educated the elite in the missionary schools and in public schools. Kwame Nkrumah from the Gold Coast (presently known as Ghana) was educated in England. Leopold Senghor of Senegal was educated in France. Dr Kamuzu Banda of Malawi was educated in Britain. Agostinho Neto, Eduardo dos Santos, and Jonas Savimbi, who were all from Angola, were educated in Portugal. This includes Amilcar Cabral from Guinea Bissau and Cape Verde, to count but a few. In South Africa we can count amongst others Dr John Dube, the first president of the ANC, and Pixley ka Seme, who were both educated in America.

All these leaders were prepared to take over from their colonial masters when independence came. We are all aware that most of the Europeans withdrew from Africa in the late fifties, sixties, and seventies. After the Africans had taken over, the only country that remained with the whites was South Africa because the Dutch had decided to make it a settler state. It took a longer time for South Africa to gain its independence from the European settlers, and as we speak, right now the recent 2012 census revealed that South Africa has about four million whites.

This counting was made eighteen years after the handing over of power from the white minority to the black majority. The countries of Africa were liberated when the Europeans designed systems that will govern indirectly for them. They had created an infrastructure linking the African economy to global markets, and it had to trade on their terms. For a number of years after the Second World War, African countries were said to owe the IMF and the World Bank billions of dollars. The debt had to be settled, and austerity measures prescribing how Africa should be governed were developed. This long and painful process after hard years of colonial rule continued unabated without any mercy.

The taking over of black people from the white administration came up with renewed hopes. A new flag was hoisted, a new president was inaugurated, and the liberation movement became the dominant party in parliament. However, a new oppression commenced. We began to notice the old ways slowly creeping back and the new constitution being redefined, and just like in the *Animal Farm* by George Orwell, we began to notice that 'some animals are more equal than others'.

In other African countries, like Congo and Ghana, they began to have tribal factions, and coups d'état were noticed. Kwame Nkrumah from Ghana was deposed, and Patrice Lumumba from Congo died in a very brutal way. He was supposed to give direction to the Congolese people, but failure to acknowledge his integrity by his fellow countrymen, like Chombe and Mobutu Sese Seko, deprived the Congolese a man of high calibre and an intelligent statesman. As a result, Congo is still trapped in the spate of violence and tribal wars to this day. The power-hungry Mobutu and Chombe collaborated with the Belgians, who were still bitter that Patrice Lumumba had facilitated their downfall, and they killed this intelligent son of the African soil.

We can count a number of other examples where African leaders turn into nasty animals after taking over from their European counterparts. Others do not break relations with their former oppressors. They simply replaced a white face with a black face, and then oppression remains. In South Africa the whites simply negotiated with the liberation movement ANC on how to reform the governing systems which discriminated black people, and then they assisted one another in governing the country. It was a negotiated settlement on how to loosen the noose on the necks of the African people. The South African ANC suffocated the voice of black intellectuals and suppressed the thinkers who could have made a meaningful contribution to the upliftment of the black masses.

They appointed uneducated people into positions of power, and cronies who have never been to school are enriched through a number of undeserved opportunities. There is public display of opulence (the buying of expensive houses, fleshy cars, designer clothing), tenderpreneurship, less work, and more drudgery. Prince Mashele, in his book *The Death of Our Society*, states, 'Fewer still want to think on behalf of our society. In fact, thinkers are despised by wealthy imbeciles.' In short, the new political dispensation is a total disappointment, and this book was written with that element of bitterness and with the aim to define the status quo as viewed by the tinted glasses of its disgruntled author.

BIBLIOGRAPHY

The Bible, King James Version.
Hitler, Adolf, *Mein Kampf*.
Johnson, R. W., *South Africa's Brave New World*.
Mashele, Prince, *The Death of Our Society*.
Zyl Slabbert, Frederik van, *The Other Side of History*.

www.ingramcontent.com/pod-product-compliance
Lightning Source LLC
Chambersburg PA
CBHW030916180526
45163CB00004B/1858